The
RELIABILITY
of the
GOSPEL
TRADITION

The
RELIABILITY
of the
GOSPEL
TRADITION

BIRGER GERHARDSSON
foreword by Donald A. Hagner

Printed in the United States of America

First printing — November 2001

"The Origins of the Gospel Tradition" was originally published in Swedish
as *Evangeliernas förhistoria* (Lund: Verbum-Håkan Ohlssons, 1977). An
English version was published as *The Origins of the Gospel Traditions*, ©
Fortress Press, 1979. Assigned 2000 to Birger Gerhardsson. "The Path of
the Gospel Tradition" was originally published in German translation as
"Der Weg der Evangelientradition" in *Das Evangelium und die Evangelien:
Vorträge vom Tübinger Symposium 1982* (ed. Peter Stuhlmacher; Tübingen:
Mohr [Siebeck], 1983). The present English version of these two works
were prepared by the author. "The Gospel Tradition" was written and pub-
lished by the author in English and distributed by a Swedish publisher
(Lund: Gleerup, 1986). For additional publication history, see the Preface.

COVER ILLUSTRATION: Jacob Jordaens (1593–1678), *The Four Evangelists*.
Louvre, Paris. Courtesy of Scala / Art Resource.

Library of Congress Cataloging-in-Publication Data

Gerhardsson, Birger.
    The reliability of the Gospel tradition / Birger Gerhardsson.
        p. cm.
    Includes bibliographical references.
    ISBN 1-56563-667-8 (pbk. : alk. paper)
    1. Bible. N.T. Gospels—Criticism, interpretation, etc.
  2. Tradition (Theology)—History of doctrines—Early church,
ca. 30–600. I. Title.
BS2555.52 .G47 2002
226'.06—dc21

                                                                    2001005962

Contents

Foreword

From the Enlightenment onwards, the question of the historical reliability of the Gospels has presented a perennial challenge to informed Christians. The typical university or seminary student, for example, upon first encountering the subject in an introductory course on the Gospels can experience something of a crisis in faith. It looks at first as though there are but two alternatives. The first is to accept the radical critical approach and then because of the resultant skepticism concerning the historical Jesus to modify and restructure one's Christian faith in a very dramatic fashion, perhaps even to reject it. The second is to retreat fearfully into a cocoon, refuse to exercise one's critical judgment altogether, finding safety in an a priori, untested view of the Gospels as, for example, inerrant documents, immune from critical judgment. It seems to come down to a simple choice between belief and unbelief.

A vibrant Christian faith, however, does not demand a sacrifice of the intellect. We believe but we also want to understand. Our faith informs our understanding, of course, but our understanding in turn must also inform our faith. Since the word of God comes to us in the form of human words, we have no option but to employ our critical judgment in the understanding of the Gospels. This is our Enlightenment heritage, with both the challenge and privilege it presents.

It can hardly be denied that there have been casualties along the way, from which we may be duly cautioned. One of the earliest radical approaches to the Gospels in the wake of the Enlightenment was that of Hermann Samuel Reimarus (1694–1768). His conclusions were so devastating to Christian faith (which he gave up) that they were published only posthumously, beginning in the 1770s, by Gotthold Ephraim Lessing in seven "Fragments."[1] Reimarus was not so much rational as rationalistic. The a priori bias of his work and its unrestrained speculation (reminiscent of some recent books on the historical Jesus) make it of little use today in understanding the Gospels. Far more influential was David Friedrich Strauss (1808–1874), whose famous *The Life of Jesus Critically Examined*[2] shook the nineteenth century as few other books did. This bombshell, first published in 1835, effectively demolished rationalistic explanations of the gospel narratives, but firmly rejected supernatural explanations too, arguing instead for an understanding of the Gospels as mythical— that is, as vehicles for a form of truth that transcends the historical. Like Reimarus, Strauss also abandoned his Christian faith. In the twentieth century, it was the highly influential Rudolf Bultmann who classically manifested skepticism concerning the historical narratives of the Gospels. For him the historicity of the gospel narratives was of no importance to Christianity. Although he maintained that we could know next to nothing about Jesus, he nevertheless wrote a book on Jesus.[3] It was, however, the kerygma of the early church alone that mattered to him, and it was unimportant whether or not there was any substantial connection between it and the historical Jesus. The negative conclusions of form criticism concerning the historicity of the gospel material came virtually to dominate New Testament scholarship through a good part of the century. Although Bultmann remained a Christian and a loyal member of the church, there can be little doubt that his work was largely destructive of Christian faith as generally formulated.

---

[1] The so-called *Wolfenbüttel Fragments,* taken from a much larger work entitled *Apology or Defense for the Rational Worshipers of God.* Some of this material is available in English translation in Reimarus, *Fragments* (ed. C. H. Talbert; Philadelphia: Fortress, 1970).

[2] The 1846 English translation (of the fourth edition) was by the famous author George Eliot. In recent times a reprint was edited by Peter C. Hodgson (Philadelphia: Fortress, 1973).

[3] *Jesus and the Word* (ET; New York: Scribner's Sons, 1958). The German original, *Jesus,* appeared in 1926 (Berlin: Deutsche Bibliothek).

Thus major figures in each of the last three centuries have articulated in powerful ways a negative assessment of the historical character of the Gospels. Today there are vocal advocates of a similar
negativism. Standing very much in the train of Reimarus, Strauss
and Bultmann, the poorly named Jesus Seminar has lately made an
enormous impact, at least in the United States. They have thrown a
question mark over the vast majority of the gospel narratives, concluding that 82 percent of the sayings ascribed to Jesus in the Gospels were not spoken by him[4] and that a great many of the deeds
attributed to him were not done by him.[5]

The Jesus Seminar is an odd phenomenon. Although they are a
relatively small number of scholars, they eagerly foist their views
upon the public as representative of true scholarship applied to the
Gospels, while failing to pay any attention to the vast majority of
mainstream critical scholars who disagree with them—indeed, not
even hinting that such scholars exist. Because in our world there is a
hunger for the new and controversial, the Jesus Seminar's views are
highly marketable and they have therefore had an impact entirely
out of proportion to their importance.

Their method is unconvincing, since they only arrive at conclusions they have assumed from the beginning, before the evidence is
examined. The first of the Seminar's methodological and programmatic presuppositions, for example, is the necessity of distinguishing
"between the historical Jesus . . . and the Christ of faith encapsulated
in the first creeds."[6] This assumes a priori that what the followers of
Jesus said about him in the Gospels and in the other New Testament
writings cannot be true to history.[7] With this comes the already
familiar reversal of the burden of proof. "It was once assumed," they
state, "that scholars had to prove the details in the Synoptic Gospels
were *not* historical . . . the gospels are now assumed to be narratives

---

[4] *The Five Gospels: The Search for the Authentic Words of Jesus* (New
York: Macmillan, 1993), 5. One of the dedicatees of the book is David
Friedrich Strauss, "who pioneered the quest of the historical Jesus."

[5] *The Acts of Jesus: The Search for the Authentic Deeds of Jesus* (ed. Robert W. Funk; San Francisco: Harper, 1998).

[6] *The Five Gospels*, 3.

[7] For this emphasis see Robert W. Funk, *Honest to Jesus: Jesus for a
New Millennium* (San Francisco: HarperSanFrancisco, 1996), passim.

in which the memory of Jesus is embellished by the mythic elements that express the church's faith in him, and by plausible fictions that enhance the telling of the gospel story for first-century listeners . . . Supposedly historical elements in these narratives must therefore be demonstrated to be so."[8] In no other field of the historical study of antiquity are historical sources subjected to such an unreasonable demand. Indeed, if this were required of all historical sources, the possibility of historical knowledge would all but disappear. The demand is altogether unreasonable and furthermore fails to appreciate the nature of historical knowledge, where in any case we cannot talk of demonstration, but only of degrees of probability.

The historicity of the Gospels thus remains under attack today as much as at any time since the Enlightenment. The Jesus Seminar is in its own way as absolute and polarized—and unconvincing—as is the fundamentalist approach at the other end of the spectrum. One might liken it to a reverse kind of fundamentalism. There is no scholarship but their scholarship, and therefore the choice is either to accept their viewpoint or to remain in what they regard as undiscerning ignorance.

But are these the only two possibilities? In finding a way between the two absolutes in the approach to the Gospels, I have personally been helped by the writings of Birger Gerhardsson, professor at the University of Lund in Sweden (now retired) and an acknowledged authority on the formation of the Gospels. I have recommended his fine little book *The Origins of the Gospel Traditions* to countless students over the years as one of the best discussions of the trustworthiness of the tradition underlying the Synoptic Gospels.[9] It was my desire to see this book—out of print now for nearly twenty years—readily available again that prompted me to approach Professor Gerhardsson about the possibility of its republication, perhaps supplemented with other writings of his along the same line.

---

[8] *The Five Gospels,* 4–5.

[9] We speak here only of the Synoptic Gospels since it is clear that the Fourth Gospel is a different kind of gospel. There the historical tradition has been worked over much more freely, and in a much more deliberately interpretive way. By that very contrast, however, the historical controls at work in the Synoptics become more conspicuous.

Twenty-five years ago Gerhardsson was addressing the negative views of the historicity of the Gospels held by form critical scholars under the influence of Bultmann. With only very minor adjustments, however, his arguments also provide an effective answer to the current claims of the Jesus Seminar and the negative assessment of the historical content of the Gospels reflected in many contemporary books on Jesus. Thus the writings made newly available in the present volume are highly relevant to the current scene.

Gerhardsson has devoted almost the whole of his academic career to the study of the oral tradition that is the basis of our canonical gospels. His groundbreaking doctoral dissertation, *Memory and Manuscript: Oral Tradition and Written Transmission in Rabbinic Judaism and Early Christianity*,[10] drew a parallel, as the subtitle suggests, between the way in which the rabbis taught their disciples and the way Jesus taught his disciples. That way involved memorization of the master's teaching. If the rabbinic disciples handed on their masters' tradition with great care, how much more the disciples of Jesus would have done so with what he taught them. And, indeed, there are indications in the synoptic tradition that Jesus formulated his teachings in memorable ways. In the concluding section of *Memory and Manuscript* Gerhardsson writes: "The implication is that the words and works of Jesus were stamped on the memories of these disciples. Remembering the attitude of Jewish disciples to their master, it is unrealistic to suppose that forgetfulness and the exercise of a pious imagination had too much hand in transforming authentic memories beyond all recognition in the course of a few short decades."[11]

Gerhardsson's argument has occasionally been unfairly dismissed by some who believe that memorization necessitates an airtight transmission down to the last syllable. But it is very important to note that never for a moment did Gerhardsson deny that the Jesus tradition had undergone interpretation, alteration, editing, adapting, and the like.

---

[10] Recently republished together with *Tradition and Transmission in Early Christianity*, with a foreword by Jacob Neusner (Grand Rapids: Eerdmans; Livonia: Dove, 1998).

[11] *Memory*, 329.

It is perfectly clear that the preserved Jesus traditions have been affected by the early church's conviction that Christ had risen from the dead, and that the Holy Spirit had come; they are likewise marked by the use which was made of them in the many-sided activity of the young church. Work on the Word has left distinct traces on these traditions. But it is one thing to state that traditions have been *marked* by the milieu through which they passed; another to claim that they simply were *created* in this secondary milieu. The evidence suggests that memories of Jesus were so clear, and the traditions with which they were connected so firmly based that there can have been relatively little scope for alteration.[12]

Gerhardsson thus does not propose an either/or but establishes a context that enables the affirmation of the basic integrity and reliability of the tradition while allowing at the same time modifications of the tradition in the postresurrection era.

This approach stands in strong contrast to that of the Jesus Seminar. Their idea of putting the sayings of Jesus in red or black (even when modified by pink and grey), depending on whether he is regarded as actually having said them or not, is absolutistic and simplistic. One gets the impression from the Seminar that if we do not have *ipsissima verba* (the very words of Jesus) we have nothing. The coloring game is silliness because it asks the wrong question. If I were to play the game, I would say that the entire corpus of the sayings of Jesus should be both black and red at the same time: black because he spoke in Aramaic while our gospels are in Greek and are not written transcripts of tape recordings (the very act of translation involves interpretation); red because the Synoptic Gospels provide us with the *ipsissima vox* (the very voice of Jesus) that is, a highly trustworthy representation of what he actually said and meant.

One fundamental weakness of the Jesus Seminar is their mistaken assessment of the nature of oral tradition. One of their methodological principles calls for "the recognition of the fundamental contrast between the oral culture (in which Jesus was at home) and a print culture (like our own)."[13] Although this simplification ignores the fact that writing and scriptures played an important role in

---

[12] *Tradition and Transmission in Early Christianity,* 43.
[13] *The Five Gospels,* 4.

Israel, and had done so for centuries, it is of course partly true. What is *not* true, however, is the general conclusion that the Seminar wants to draw from this "principle," namely that material cannot be accurately handed on in oral tradition. What is forgotten here is that the effectiveness of oral transmission in the first century must not be judged by the standards of our day.

Without any careful examination of oral tradition in the time and context of Jesus, of the sort that Professor Gerhardsson has done so well, the Jesus Seminar thus foolishly compares oral tradition to modern situations where our memories can be shown to be faulty. They talk about our inability to retell a joke in the same words as we first heard it; they tell us from modern psychological study that short-term memory can retain only seven items at a time and that "people forget the exact wording of a particular statement after only sixteen syllables intervene between the original statement and the request to recall that wording."[14] I have even heard the appeal to the parlor game where a story is whispered from person to person around a circle and then there is great laughter at how different the story told by the final person is from what was originally told. All this appeals to the common idea that memory cannot be trusted, and after all, it is emphasized, the tradition that comes into our gospels was in oral form for at least some thirty years before it was written down.

One of the great virtues of Gerhardsson's work is that it takes us back to the historical context in which the Gospels were written. Two major points emphasized by Gerhardsson and ignored by the Jesus Seminar deserve emphasis here. First, memories in the ancient world were much more practiced and hence more efficient than memories in the modern world are. Education was often by rote memorization. It is particularly relevant to note that rabbinic students were able to learn by heart and retain enormous amounts of material delivered to them by their masters. The model of rabbi and disciples, although not exactly the same in every detail, was very similar to that of Jesus and his disciples. Second, one must remember the high esteem in which the disciples held Jesus and the effect this would have had on their perception of the importance of what

---

[14] *The Five Gospels*, 27–28.

Jesus was teaching them. What he taught them was from the beginning holy speech, far from being anything ordinary or of little consequence. They would therefore have taken special care in the mastering, maintenance, and transmission of this tradition. So modern parallels appealing to mundane matters have little meaning when applied to the gospel tradition, and the arguments of the Jesus Seminar cannot be used to undercut the reliability of the sayings tradition in the Synoptic Gospels.

A negative view of the historicity of the Gospels obviously has enormous consequences for how one understands Jesus. Indeed, if the Jesus portrayed in the Synoptic Gospels is a fiction of the gospel writers, then one is forced to search for other frameworks and paradigms by which to understand him.[15] In the last decade or two we have witnessed a growing number of books on the so-called historical Jesus. (By this what is often meant is the "real" Jesus rather than the one portrayed in the Gospels.) To the extent that these books move away from the information and perspectives contained in the Gospels, they are bound to mislead readers.

In the final estimate of the Jesus Seminar, Jesus was a laconic sage, a kind of secular iconoclast who traveled about teaching a proverbial wisdom that often disturbed the religious establishment. I am reminded of Professor Birger Pearson's satirical summary of the Jesus Seminar: "A group of secularized theologians and secular academics went seeking a secular Jesus, and they found him! They think they found him, but, in fact, they created him. Jesus the 'party animal' whose zany wit and caustic humor would enliven an otherwise dull cocktail party—this is the product of the Jesus Seminar's six years' research."[16]

---

[15] Gerhardsson makes a similar point about much recent parable interpretation in his Society of New Testament Studies presidential address of 1990, "If We Do Not Cut the Parables Out of Their Frames," *New Testament Studies* 37 (1991): 321–35.

[16] "The Gospel according to the Jesus Seminar," *Religion* 25 (1995): 317–38, now in expanded form as chapter 2 of Pearson's *The Emergence of the Christian Religion: Essays on Early Christianity* (Harrisburg: Trinity Press International, 1997). See too his "An Exposé of the Jesus Seminar," in *Dialog* 37 (1998): 28–35. For other critiques of the Jesus Seminar, see especially R. B. Hays, "The Corrected Jesus," *First Things* 43 (1994): 43–48; L. T.

Now the founder of the Seminar, Robert W. Funk, has his own book out on Jesus entitled *Honest to Jesus: Jesus for a New Millennium,*[17] in which he describes Jesus as a secular sage and social critic who through satire and humor opposed the religious authorities in favor of the marginalized of society, especially the poor. The cochair of the Seminar, John Dominic Crossan, is also the author of a major book on the historical Jesus, *The Historical Jesus: The Life of a Mediterranean Jewish Peasant.*[18] The one key word missing from the subtitle to the book that is important to Crossan's picture of Jesus is the word "cynic." Jesus was critical of the status quo and proclaimed the radical alternative of a "brokerless" and "egalitarian" kingdom—a kingdom without mediators, without hierarchy, and without prejudice against sinners. In the final assessment, Jesus is a radical, antiestablishment, countercultural social reformer.

We need not mention here the flock of other Jesus books along similar lines. The Jesus Seminar seems unaware that their "first general rule of evidence" cuts in more than one direction. That rule— "Beware of finding a Jesus entirely congenial to you"[19]—applies equally well to their view of Jesus. Is it not the New Testament's view of Jesus that is uncongenial to them?

Gerhardsson's view of the trustworthy character of the Gospels can deliver us from much of the nonsense in modern portrayals of Jesus. Ben F. Meyer has rightly concluded that Gerhardsson's perspective, if heeded, could

> signal an era of renewed confidence in historical-Jesus research. We would then become far less liable to the temptation to be stunningly original. Given Gerhardsson's account of the origin of the gospel tradition, such original constructs as a political, noneschatological Jesus

---

Johnson, *The Real Jesus: The Misguided Quest for the Historical Jesus and the Truth of the Traditional Gospels* (San Francisco: Harper, 1995); N. T. Wright, "Five Gospels but No Gospel: Jesus and the Seminar," *Crisis in Christology: Essays in Quest of Resolution* (ed. W. R. Farmer; Livonia: Dove, 1995), 115–57.

[17] See above, n. 7.

[18] San Francisco: Harper San Francisco, 1991. More recently a short, popular version of the same: *Jesus: A Revolutionary Biography* (San Francisco: Harper Collins, 1994).

[19] *The Five Gospels,* 5.

heading "the peace party" in Judaism, or a deceptively peaceful revolutionary giving the world antiestablishment wisdom in parable
form, or a Jesus intent on including the wicked in his kingdom without requiring their conversion, would likely die unborn. For it is difficult, if not impossible, to conjure up this combination: on the one
hand, commitment to an account of tradition under the care of "eyewitnesses" who had now become "ministers of the word" and, on the
other hand, these stunningly original views of Jesus.[20]

Most people seem to know that there is something wrong with
the Jesus Seminar's excessively negative estimate of the historical
worth of the Gospels, just as they know that the fundamentalistic
view of the Gospels is also inadequate. For these thinking Christians,
as well as for theological students encountering the challenge head
on, Gerhardsson is an intelligent, insightful, and authoritative guide
to understanding what lies behind the Gospels and what makes
them what they are.

In the current climate of skepticism I know of nothing more
helpful than Birger Gerhardsson's writings, and that is why I am particularly delighted that the pieces that compose the present volume
are again available in print. New generations of students deserve to
have them, not merely because they ultimately vindicate the church's
estimate of Jesus, but because they are true to the nature of the Gospels themselves and to the purpose of those who wrote them.

DONALD A. HAGNER
Fuller Theological Seminary
Pasadena, Calif.

---

[20] "Some Consequences of Birger Gerhardsson's Account of the Origins of the Gospel Tradition," *Jesus and the Oral Gospel Tradition* (JSNTSSup
4; ed. Henry Wansbrough; Sheffield: Sheffield Academic Press, 1991),
424–40, at 428–29.

Preface

In the spring 1976, I was invited by a German theological society (*Pfarrer-Gebets-Bruderschaft*) to lecture to German students of theology. The overarching theme on that occasion was the value of the Gospels as historical sources, and the place was Holzhausen, not far from Marburg, the university city of the renowned Rudolf Bultmann. My lectures were published in 1977 with the title *Die Anfänge der Evangelientradition*[1] and appeared the same year in Swedish under the title *Evangeliernas förhistoria,*[2] as well as later on in English, French, Danish, Italian, and Spanish (1977–80).

The lectures in Holzhausen were held at a time when the so-called form-critical school *(Formgeschichte)* still had a safe hold on gospel research in Germany, with a wide hearing even in other countries. Its influence was, however, on the decrease. The situation was different fifteen years earlier, when my doctoral dissertation *Memory and Manuscript: Oral Tradition and Written Transmission in Rabbinic Judaism and Early Christianity* (1961)[3] appeared. That book received very severe criticism from the form critics, something which only partly was due to the fact that it was written in a somewhat pointed way. The book aroused a lively debate and I felt called upon to publish a follow-up booklet in which I tried to remove misunderstanding and meet objections against my approach.

---

[1] Glauben und Denken 919; Wuppertal: Brockhaus.
[2] Lund: Verbum-H. Ohlsson.
[3] ASNU 22; Lund: C. W. K. Gleerup; Copenhagen: E. Munksgaard.

The name of this booklet was *Tradition and Transmission in Early Christianity* (1964).[4]

"The Origins of the Gospel Tradition," which is now reprinted in the present volume, is the English translation of the Holzhausen lectures. The time and the place of the lectures explain why the presentation is angled as it is. My task was to discuss the origins and earliest history of the gospel tradition. The audience was educated in the form-critical theories with a very skeptical opinion of the reliability of the Gospels. It is against this approach that I conduct my argumentation. If it had been today, I would have devoted more space to the interesting changes which seem to have occurred in the Jesus traditions between the Master's ministry and the emergence of our four gospels. The texts have, as we know, to some extent become colored by the experiences the Christians had and the insights they gained after the death of Jesus and the breakthrough of the resurrection belief, something I have tried to elucidate in other connections over the years. Today I would also have reminded my listeners of the *problematic* character of all formation of tradition, even within the church.

The faculties of theology in Sweden have for many years had good cooperation with their German colleagues in Tübingen. As to my dissertation, one of the two New Testament professors at the Protestant faculty of Theology in Tübingen, Ernst Käsemann, wrote a caustic review, one of the most negative presentations my book received (1963). The other New Testament professor, Otto Michel, also reviewed the book (1964), but in an appreciative way.

It was presumably at the instigation of Professor Michel that I was invited to Holzhausen in 1976; we gave lectures there, both of us. Dr. Michel also wrote (together with his colleague in Wuppertal, Klaus Haacker) the preface to the German edition of my lectures.

In November 1980, I gave guest lectures in Tübingen, this time invited by Dr. Käsemann's successor, Peter Stuhlmacher. Two years later he organized an international symposium on the theme "The Gospel and the Gospels." The lectures and discussions on this occasion were characterized by a balanced view of tradition. The contributions were

---

[4]ConNT 20; Lund: Gleerup; Copenhagen: Munksgaard; now Stockholm: Almqvist & Wiksell International.

edited—by Dr. Stuhlmacher—in a massive volume with the title
*Das Evangelium und die Evangelien: Vorträge vom Tübinger Sympo-
sium 1982.*[5] My essay had the title "Der Weg der Evangelientradition."
The book appeared in 1991 in an English translation as well.[6] My contribution, "The Path of the Gospel Tradition," is now reprinted in the
present volume, this time much better translated.

An important dissertation had been ventilated and published in
Tübingen before the Tübinger Symposium, Rainer Riesner's *Jesus als
Lehrer: Eine Untersuchung zum Ursprung der Evangelien-Überlieferung.*[7]
Riesner—who was present in Holzhausen 1976—complements
Memory and Manuscript by elucidating the transmission which
occurred in broad, popular contexts in Israel: in homes, elementary
schools, and synagogal activities. His contribution refutes a point of
view which the Jewish-American rabbinist Jacob Neusner had put forward against my dissertation, namely that the rabbinic methods of
transmission were but academic specialties. Riesner collects, furthermore, from ancient Israel and the world around it much pre-Christian
evidence that the methods of the rabbis were mainly old devices of
teaching and transmission, which only needed to be refined. In that
way he refutes the second main point of criticism against my dissertation, advanced by Dr. Neusner and others, to wit, that the rabbis after
A.D. 70 created new methods, which did not exist in the time of Jesus
and his apostles. Riesner's dissertation has received great attention; it
has appeared in three German editions (the latest in 1988), and the
promised English translation is long overdue.

In April 1984, a lengthy symposium held in Jerusalem—"Symposium de interpretatione evangeliorum"—focused upon the question of the genetic relations between the three Synoptic Gospels
(Matthew, Mark, and Luke). The meeting had been well prepared
by three research teams—each one representing an important
approach to the synoptic question (the Two Document Hypothesis,
the Two Gospel Hypothesis and the Multiple Stage Hypothesis)—
and by individual scholars elucidating complementary aspects. All

---

[5] WUNT 28; Tübingen: Mohr (Siebeck), 1983.
[6] *The Gospel and the Gospels* (ed. P. Stuhlmacher; Grand Rapids: Eerdmans, 1991).
[7] WUNT[2] 7; Tübingen: Mohr (Siebeck), 1981.

the papers had been distributed in advance, so that the discussions could start immediately each time, after only a short introduction. One of the main concerns of the meeting was to point out areas in need of further research. My own task on this occasion was to discuss the oral prehistory of the gospel texts. I now had the opportunity to present an analysis of the anatomy of the early Christian tradition, so to speak: what it was, in its different dimensions, and how it functioned on its way from Jesus to the evangelists. I developed here my approach to the problem of tradition in a more discursive and explicit way than earlier. The documents from the symposium were published by David L. Dungan in 1990 under the title *The Interrelations of the Gospels*.[8] In the meantime, some of us had already published our papers separately. My own contribution, e.g., had appeared as a booklet with the title *The Gospel Tradition* in Sweden in 1986.[9] This text is the third item reprinted in the present volume.

The dissertation *Memory and Manuscript* was my basic study of the theme of tradition and transmission in ancient Judaism and early Christianity. The book ended with a short chapter sketching the path of the gospel tradition from Jesus to the completed Gospels, as I imagined it at that stage. I did not even begin the comprehensive task of analyzing the concrete material in the Gospels from my point of departure—against the background of early Christianity's "work with the word of the Lord." I have, however, dealt a good deal with that task since then, in a long series of contributions. I started with the somewhat peculiar text on how Jesus was put to the test by the devil before his public ministry in Israel, according to Matthew and Luke.[10] After that I examined a number of early Christian pericopes,

---

[8] BETL 95; Leuven: Leuven University Press & Peeters.

[9] ConBNT 15; Lund: Gleerup; now Stockholm: Almqvist & Wiksell International.

[10] *The Testing of God's Son (Matt 4:1–11 & Par): An Analysis of an Early Christian Midrash* (ConBNT 2:1; Lund: Gleerup, 1965; now Stockholm: Almqvist & Wiksell International). The substance of the most important of the yet unpublished chapters of the book (ch. 7) is printed as an article in German, "Gottes Sohn als Diener Gottes," in *Studia theologica* 27 (1973): 73–106, and in my volume *The Shema in the New Testament: Deut 6:4–5 in Significant Passages* (Lund: Novapress, 1996), 139–72.

where one can see that Israel's ancient creed, the Shema, including the greatest commandment in God's law, determines the line of thought and the design of the pericope.[11] I have also analyzed all the synoptic parables, which I classify as narrative meshalim, and especially the parables of the synoptic parable chapter (Matt 13 and parallels).[12] I have studied all the material in Matthew which concerns the mighty acts of Jesus,[13] and in addition the prehistory in Matthew, the passion narrative, and the resurrection stories.[14] As to the logia material (the aphoristic meshalim), I have so far not, however, been able to examine more than a limited number of sayings.[15] Here very much remains to be done, and my own contributions hereafter will be few.

After a series of exegetical conferences on the synoptic question, a two-part symposium was held in Dublin, Ireland, in 1989 and

---

[11] Seventeen of these studies, originally published one by one in scattered journals and festschrifts, have been collected in my book *The Shema in the New Testament* (n. 11).

[12] All the parables are analyzed in the article "Illuminating the Kingdom: Narrative Meshalim in the Synoptic Gospels," in *Jesus and the Oral Gospel Tradition* (JSNTSup 64; Sheffield: JSOT Press, 1991), 266–309. On the parable chapter see "The Parable of the Sower and Its Interpretation," *New Testament Studies* 14 (1967–1968): 165–93, and "The Seven Parables in Matthew XIII," *New Testament Studies* 19 (1972–1973): 16–37. More exhaustive is my book *Jesu liknelser: En genomlysning* (Lund: Novapress, 1999).

[13] *The Mighty Acts of Jesus according to Matthew* (Scripta minora 1978–1979, 5; Lund: Gleerup, 1979), completed with the article "Mighty Acts and Rule of Heaven: 'God Is with Us,'" in *The Shema in the New Testament,* 187–201. More exhaustive is the Swedish version of this study, *Jesu maktgärningar i Matteusevangeliet* (Lund: Novapress, 1991).

[14] See, *inter alia,* my contribution "Ur Matteusevangeliet" (commentary on chs. 1–2, 5–7, 26–28), in *Ur Nya testamentet* (ed. L. Hartman; 2d ed.; Lund: Gleerup, 1972), 108–201; the article "Gottes Sohn als Diener Gottes," and further "Kristi uppståndelse—de bibliska vittnesbörden," *Din uppståndelse bekänner vi* (ed. E. Franck; Stockholm: Verbum, 1988), 24–61, as well as "Mark and the Female Witnesses," *Dumu-E₂-Dub-ba-a: Studies in Honor of Ake W. Sjöberg* (ed. H. Behrens et al.; Philadelphia: Occasional Publications of the S. N. Kramer Fund 11, 1989), 217–26.

[15] See, e.g., my comments on the Sermon on the Mount in "Ur Matteusevangeliet," 125–50; "Salt and Sacrifice: A Cryptic Mission Word in Matthew (5:13a)," in *The Sum of Our Choices: Essays in Honour of Eric J. Sharpe* (ed. A. Sharma; Atlanta: Scholars Press, 1996), 265–76; and some articles in *The Shema in the New Testament.*

Gazzada, Italy, in 1990 on the theme "Oral Tradition before, in, and outside the Gospels." At these two meetings a number of scholars discussed the oral Jesus tradition behind the four gospels, behind the Pauline letters and the *Didache,* and this in the light of recent results from tradition research within other disciplines. The thirteen introductory papers from the symposium were published in 1991 by Dom Henry Wansbrough with the title *Jesus and the Oral Gospel Tradition.*[16] For my part I addressed the synoptic parables under the heading "Illuminating the Kingdom: Narrative Meshalim in the Synoptic Gospels."[17]

Some years ago the tradition problem was enriched by an extensive and solid investigation, written by my pupil Samuel Byrskog, *Jesus the Only Teacher: Didactic Authority and Transmission in Ancient Israel, Ancient Judaism, and the Matthean Community.* The author shows how Jesus is presented as teacher in the Gospel of Matthew and how the treatment of the transmitted material has been influenced by the conviction that Jesus is "the only teacher" of the church. Dr. Byrskog has brought the study of the early Christian Jesus tradition a clear step forward.[18]

In 1998 a third edition of *Memory and Manuscript,* with the follow-up booklet *Tradition and Transmission in Early Christianity* in the same volume, was published in the United States.[19] The book starts with two new texts, one written by me, the other by one of my sharpest critics, Professor Jacob Neusner. My preface contains an account of the origin and aim of my dissertation, of the discussion around it, and of my further work on the early Christian tradition. In his generous foreword Dr. Neusner then recommends my book unreservedly, at the same time apologizing for the negative criticism

---

[16] JSNTSup 64; Sheffield: JSOT Press.

[17] See above, n. 12.

[18] ConBNT 24; Stockholm: Almqvist & Wiksell International, 1994. See now also Byrskog's *Story as History—History as Story: The Gospel Tradition in the Context of Ancient Oral History* (WUNT 123; Tübingen: Mohr [Siebeck], 2000). See also S. Westerholm, *Jesus and Scribal Authority* (ConBNT 10; Lund: Gleerup, 1978).

[19] *Memory and Manuscript: Oral Tradition and Written Transmission in Rabbinic Judaism and Early Christianity* with *Tradition and Transmission in Early Christianity* (Grand Rapids: Eerdmans; Livonia: Dove, 1998).

he leveled against it in his youth. It is not easy for a scholar to admit being wrong earlier; Jack Neusner has the moral courage to do so.

The present volume contains reprints of three of my studies of the early Christian tradition. As I have already indicated above, the texts have originated at different points of time and in different circumstances. They also have a different character. "The Origins of the Gospel Tradition," from 1976, gives a popular review of the question to what extent the New Testament evangelists enable us to hear the voice of Jesus. The basic question is: Was the tradition from Jesus and about Jesus preserved in a reliable way, and are the records of the Gospels trustworthy? Second, "The Path of the Gospel Tradition," from 1983, contains a critical discussion of the approach of the form-critical school to the problem of the early Christian tradition, ending with an alternative sketch of the path of the tradition. In the third study, "The Gospel Tradition," from 1986, I have tried to give a rather detailed picture of the different aspects of the early Christian tradition and of the transmission of it as well as an assessment of the reliability of the four oldest of the extant written records.

Two of the texts are here reprinted in their original form, apart from some minor stylistic improvements and updated literature references in some footnotes. Within brackets I also add a few new pieces of information. As for the article "The Path of the Gospel Tradition," however, a thorough renovation of the earlier translation (published in 1991) has been necessary, since it was very poor and quite often misleading.

Many scholars confine themselves today to studying the New Testament documents as *texts*—their nature, structure, content, and way of functioning, as well as their readers' reading and reception of them—and to expressing an opinion about their reliability as historical sources without discussing the question how the material may have been preserved during the decades between the Master's ministry in Israel and the evangelists' writings. They fail to give any attention to two centuries of assiduous attempts to elucidate how the sayings of Jesus and the memories of his ministry were preserved during the first decades of the church. To me it seems clear that the question whether the New Testament documents give us a historically reliable picture of Jesus of Nazareth, cannot be answered without a thorough study of the early Christian tradition problem. Although it is a difficult issue, we must do what we can.

For my part, I have become convinced that we can hear the voice of Jesus himself in the Gospels. His pronouncements and the narratives about his actions have been interpreted and clarified by his disciples, but they reach us nevertheless in a reliable form. These small texts have been handed down to posterity by devoted and faithful adherents who wanted nothing other than to receive the message of their master, and that in such a way that they would be able to preserve it and clarify it to others, so that they might know as much as possible about Jesus Christ, the crucified, resurrected, and living Lord of the church.

My old friend Donald Hagner—an American of Swedish extraction on the paternal side—has taken the initiative to produce this book. He has also seen to the negotiations with the publishers and spent considerable time on the manuscript, improved the translation, checked bibliographical data, and so forth. I thank him warmly for his brotherly help, this time as well as on many earlier occasions given gladly.

BIRGER GERHARDSSON
Lund, September 2001

I

✿

The Origins of the Gospel Tradition

INTRODUCTION

Research has expended enormous effort and great ingenuity in order to enable us, if at all possible, to work out the historical truth about Jesus of Nazareth. Do our sources—and above all the first three gospels—provide us with a fairly dependable picture of Jesus: who he was, what he proclaimed, what he did, and what form his fate took?

During the nineteenth century scholars worked with these questions primarily in a literary-critical manner. They sought to get a firm hold on the oldest information in the Gospels by getting at the *literary sources* the evangelists had built upon. Gradually, however, they began to see that this would not produce the desired results, for it is obvious that there was a period of *oral tradition* which lay between Jesus' ministry and the earliest written records. What had happened to these remembrances during this preliterary period?

A bold step forward was taken in this area in the years right after World War I. The new effort came to be known as the form-critical school, and its pioneers included Martin Dibelius *(Die Formgeschichte des Evangeliums),*[1] Rudolf Bultmann *(Die Geschichte der synoptischen Tradition),*[2] and Karl Ludwig Schmidt *(Der Rahmen*

---

[1] Tübingen: Mohr (Siebeck), 1921; ET *From Tradition to Gospel* (trans. B. Lee Wolfe; New York: Scribner's Sons, 1934).

[2] FRLANT 29; Göttingen: Vandenhoeck & Ruprect, 1921; 2d ed., 1931; ET *History of the Synoptic Tradition* (trans. J. Marsh; based on the 3d

der Geschichte Jesu).[3] Applying insights which had been provided initially by researchers of antiquity, folklore specialists, and Old Testament exegetes, these scholars sought to clarify the oral tradition in the early church. They sorted out the gospel material into different types of form (*Gattungen*), and sought to place these into the context in which they were thought to have arisen and been used in the activity of the early church (i.e., the material's *Sitz im Leben*). These scholars further wrote the history of these traditions and set forth judgments concerning their historical value. Bultmann in particular showed great skepticism here. The results had a great effect on gospel research in Germany. In other countries too the scientific study of the Gospels was influenced more by form criticism than by any other scholarly conclusions in the past fifty years. This has happened even though much of the work of the form-critical school has been hotly debated.

This is not the place to provide a closer look at the presuppositions, methods, and results of the form-critical school. What I intend to do here is to present a brief description of how I, for my part, look upon the question of the gospel tradition's origin and history from the time of Jesus to the appearance of our written gospels.

My chief objection to the form-critical scholars—whom I agree with in part, but in part decidedly differ from—is that their work is not sufficiently *historical.* They do not show sufficient energy in anchoring the question of the origin of the gospel tradition within the framework of the question concerning how holy, authoritative tradition was transmitted in the Jewish milieu of Palestine and elsewhere at the time of the New Testament. This must surely be the starting point if one wants to understand the origins of the early Christian tradition historically.

The subject of the following presentation is therefore the origins of the gospel material and the history of its transmission, or, in other words, the prehistory of the written gospels (especially the Synoptics). I shall approach the problem as one would in secular his-

---

German edition; Oxford: Blackwell, 1963; New York: Harper & Row, 1968).

[3] *Der Rahmen der Geschichte Jesu: Literarkritische Untersuchungen zur ältesten Jesusüberlieferung* (Berlin: Trowitzsch & Sohn, 1919).

toriography. Theological viewpoints will be suggested only in passing. To prevent misunderstandings I should, however, say that an investigation of the origins of the Gospels with the methods of secular history can certainly produce important results for New Testament *theology*, but at the same time one cannot base theology on these results directly. New Testament theology must reasonably begin with a consideration of *the Christian faith's original meaning and content*, not with questions regarding the origins of the basic source material. On the other hand, historical questions cannot be answered by theological argumentation.

Since the following material was originally presented to German students of theology, I have not found it necessary to define in more detail the form-critical viewpoint which I accept in part and reject in part, nor the exegetical-historical background in general. It also explains why I have not taken up a number of basic questions of scientific and historical nature, questions one certainly cannot ignore in dealing with problems of this kind. Other lecturers dealt with these matters at Holzhausen.

Finally, the lecture form also explains why I so seldom identify sources and literary references. For support of my position I would refer the reader to two of my books, *Memory and Manuscript: Oral Tradition and Written Transmission in Rabbinic Judaism and Early Christianity*[4] and *Tradition and Transmission in Early Christianity*.[5] Both books contain ample references to source materials as well as scholarly literature. I might also point out that in both of these youthful works I often quite deliberately expressed myself a bit pointedly. A number of pertinent works will also be mentioned in the other articles of the present book.

I. JEWISH TRADITIONALISM

Discovery and research in the last generations have made it clear to us that Judaism in Palestine at the beginning of our era was

---

[4] ASNU 22; Lund: Gleerup, Copenhagen: Munksgaard, 1961, 2d ed. 1964.

[5] ConNT 20; Lund: Gleerup, 1964. [The two books have now been reprinted jointly (Grand Rapids: Eerdmans; Livonia: Dove, 1998).]

much less homogeneous than was previously known. Many dispa-
rate tendencies and groups existed. They did not all think alike.
Nonetheless, it is proper to speak of Judaism as a characteristic entity
and to point to certain qualities which united the different Jewish
groups and tendencies. One must naturally draw a line somewhere. I
do not, for example, include those Jews who had gone so far in the
direction of assimilation to the surrounding culture that they no
longer had their sons circumcised.

One characteristic which united all Jewish groups was the
conviction that Israel was God's chosen people, a people to whom
it had pleased God to give a special standing among the nations by
entering into a covenant with them. Because this covenant had
been entered in the past, had been made between God and the people's ancestors, the terms of the covenant existed as *tradition*. At the
beginning of our era monotheism was firmly established among
the Jews. Other gods held little attraction. The Jews maintained
that they were in covenant with the one true God; the God of their
fathers was for them the only true God. They sought no new, radical revelations to replace the old. What they wanted to know was
how the inherited divine revelation was to be understood in the
here and now. There were of course groups that were drawn to new
signs and revelations—apocalyptic and prophetic groups—but
even these did not want to break with the old. It was typical, for example, that the Qumran community expected that the new revelations would be found *in* the Torah, that is, in the ancient holy
scriptures.

That binding religious inheritance from the fathers, which
served as a source of inspiration and a binding norm for both communal and individual life, was identified by the inclusive term
Torah. This word *Tōrāh*, which we usually render "the Law," actually
has a much broader content than this translation would suggest. It
points to the entire revelation and instruction which Israel's God has
given to his people. All pious groups in Israel wished to be faithful to
the Torah. They might have varied opinions about Torah's character
and content and scope, but all were united in their pride and joy in
Torah, and in their recognition of its binding nature as a norm for
living. It has been said that Judaism had become *Torah-centric* (Wil-
liam Farmer).

For the dominant element of Jewish society, the Pharisaic-rabbinical element, Torah included Israel's national, binding cultural inheritance in its entirety. One could suggest a pedagogical simplification and say that Torah functioned in three external forms or dimensions: (1) as verbal tradition, (2) as practical tradition, and (3) as institutional tradition.

By *verbal* tradition I refer to words and texts, either as written in books or imprinted on the mind (or both), that is, written and oral tradition. By *practical* tradition I refer to inherited, binding patterns of living: normative conduct impressed upon the people by those in positions of authority through deeds and through verbal instruction, conduct which was learned by imitation and listening. By *institutional* tradition I refer to the institutions and establishments that generation after generation supported, for example, the temple and the synagogues, or such objects as the inscriptions on the doorposts, phylacteries, tassels on cloaks, and so on.[6]

Much could be said about this comprehensive and highly diversified tradition which in its wholeness possesses religious authority, and about its varied components, as well as about its transmission from generation to generation. But I must limit myself to certain aspects presented in a brief and sketchy form.

How did it happen that this traditionalism grew so strongly in Israel in the centuries around the beginning of our era? I have already suggested that the embryo of Jewish traditionalism is to be found in the covenant concept itself. In the reports of how God enters into a covenant with father Abraham we note that this covenant is not only to involve him but also his "seed," his descendants. He is to direct his children and his "house" to hold to God's way and to live justly and righteously (Gen 18:19). And in the description of how this covenant is consummated at Sinai we note the same thing. The generation of Israelites then living is obligated to make known to its children and grandchildren all that the covenant includes (e.g., Deut 4 and 6).

---

[6] I have later on found that one ought to make a distinction between institutions and things and speak of four dimensions: verbal, practical, institutional, and material tradition. See *The Gospel Tradition,* sect. I (below).

During the exile the Jews' religious and national uniqueness was threatened. Such threats served to make the national inheritance more precious, and its maintenance an even greater concern (cf., e.g., Ezra 7:10, 21–26). This development reached its zenith a couple of centuries later. After Alexander the Great's victory at Issos (333 B.C.), Hellenistic culture infiltrated Palestine and was accepted by many Jewish families.[7] When Palestine came under Seleucid domination (198 B.C.) this tendency increased. The climax was reached when the Seleucid king, Antiochus Epiphanes, abetted the process of Hellenization with threats and violence (167 B.C.). He attempted, by decree and by threats of extreme sanctions, to use his power to hellenize Judaism in its entirety: politically, culturally, and religiously.

There were of course a number of Jews who gave in to these royal threats. But others reacted in a different spirit to the foreign despot. Their identity, their distinctive character, was threatened at the core. An intense opposition came to life. Loyalty to that which was Jewish flamed up. For the Jews who became involved in this reaction all things native and inherited became holy and binding: not only the fathers' faith and ethos, but all else that their fathers had maintained: the Law, the customs, the institutions. The land and the language of their fathers, indeed all things Jewish, had to be defended. Zeal (in Greek, *zēlos*) for such things now became an ideal. The books of the Maccabees give us an eloquent description of the situation.

It is highly possible that the term *Judaism* (in Greek, *ioudaïsmos*) was coined in this very context as the opposite of *Hellenism* (in Greek, *hellēnismos*). The word *ioudaïsmos* first appears in 2 Maccabees (2:21; 8:1; 14:38).

Some Jews took up arms in order to protect their holy heritage. Others carried on a spiritual war, a religious cultural struggle. In both instances the Jews strove earnestly for their fathers' God and his Torah; their zeal just took different forms.

---

[7] See M. Hengel, *Judentum und Hellenismus* (2d rev. ed.; WUNT 10; Tübingen: Mohr [Siebeck], 1973), 120–52; ET *Judaism and Hellenism* (trans. J. Bowden; 2 vols.; Philadelphia: Fortress, 1974). See also idem, *Juden, Griechen, und Barbaren: Aspekte der Hellenisierung des Judentums in vorchristlicher Zeit* (SBS 76; Stuttgart: KBW Verlag, 1976); ET *Jews, Greeks, and Barbarians* (trans. J. Bowden; Philadelphia: Fortress, 1980).

II. MASTER AND DISCIPLES

It was during this cultural struggle that Jewish traditionalism, with its unbending opposition to all forms of adaptation and assimilation, began to take on its uncompromising quality. And it was within the context of this development that the ancient Jewish school system took shape. In the Greek world the schools were an effective means of spreading and establishing Hellenistic culture. If we can believe the books of the Maccabees, there were Hellenistic schools in Palestine during the second century before Christ; there was even a Hellenistic *gymnasion* for young men in Jerusalem itself (cf. 1 Macc 1:14; 2 Macc 4:9). About that time the Jews began to set up their own schools in an effort to steel their youth against the blandishments of Hellenism. These Jewish schools were similar in some respects to the Hellenistic schools, but their purpose was different. They were designed above all to convey to their young the pure inheritance of the ancient Jewish fathers, and to form (or socialize) them into true Israelites, faithful to the traditions and life-style of the fathers. There was really but one subject in the curriculum, but that one subject included everything: Torah.

In this picture of a Torah-centric Judaism we also see that it is markedly *patriarchal*. "The fathers" play a leading role as authorities and teachers. That is true both of the family fathers in the individual houses and of the fathers of the people, the "elders," that is, the persons of honor. The leading men were always of a respectable age, and it was these who acted as the authoritative representatives of the heritage of the fathers.

Among these persons of honor are some who are especially significant, to wit, *experts* of various kinds: those who, because they have grown up in a certain set of circumstances or have received a special training, are experts in certain facets of the inherited tradition. For example, there are those who have mastered the texts of the Holy Writings, and who now gather young men around them in schools of various sizes. The priests are another example; they have learned from older, experienced priests with many years of service in the temple, and as a result have become experts themselves in carrying out the various aspects of the temple ministry. Then too, there are those who have become specialists in the application of the Law.

There are also teachers of wisdom of different kinds, the successors of the makers of proverbs (the *moshelim*) in ancient Israel, reminiscent of the popular philosophers in the Hellenistic culture. Such men as these now stood out as significant *witnesses* to the ancient heritage; they were now able to *testify* to the wisdom and the way of life of the fathers. We can also mention here prophetic figures and workers of miracles. The distinction between prophets and teachers was rather nebulous in the ancient world. Prophets too had their disciples, the "sons of the prophets." In the intertestamental literature, in the historical writings of Josephus, in the New Testament, and above all in the rabbinical literature, we meet these various Torah authorities, surrounded by their disciples and supporters.

Inasmuch as knowledge is something imparted, it must be sought where it can be found. To learn Torah one must go to a teacher. Students flock around their teachers. And such a group formation—teachers and their students—becomes something of an extended family. The teacher is the spiritual father, the students his spiritual children. They spend their time with him, they follow him ("walk after" him, in Hebrew, *hālak achare*), they serve him. The house where he dwells, whether it is in fact his own or belongs to a patron, is also their house. It has been pointed out that the leading schools of the New Testament period are highly concrete realities. "Hillel's house" and "Shammai's house" are designations which refer not only to sizable spiritual families, but also to the very buildings where they met together.

Students learn much of the Torah tradition by *listening:* by listening to their teacher and his more advanced students as well as by asking questions and making contributions of their own within the bounds prescribed by modesty and etiquette. But they also learn a great deal by simply *observing:* with attentive eyes they observe all that the teacher does and then proceed to imitate him. Torah is above all a holy, authoritative attitude toward life and a way of life. Because this is true, much can be learned simply by watching and imitating those who are knowledgeable.

In the Talmud, that miscellany of material collected from discussions held in the rabbinical schools, we can see how the participants quote what various teachers have said. Someone has heard rabbi so-and-so say this or that. But we also note here references to what the learned men actually have done: "I saw rabbi so-and-so do thus and so." The rabbinical tradition preserves examples of how bright and eager students followed their teacher's actions even in the most private situations, motivated by the belief that "This has to do with Torah, and I want to learn!" An amusing story tells how two students one evening hid themselves in their teacher's bedroom where he slept with his wife. When the teacher suddenly discovered them he was naturally furious, but they defended themselves by arguing in all innocence that this too involved Torah, and they wanted to learn.

Such examples indicate to us that the person involved learns not simply the texts and the obligatory way of life cultivated in a certain school, but also the spirit and atmosphere created by a teacher and his students working together in fellowship. It is interesting to note how certain visible and audible characteristics come to identify those who belong to a certain school. Certain peculiarities in their conduct, or certain manners of speaking, suffice to indicate that an individual belongs to Hillel's school or to Shammai's school, or whatever. The initiated observer can thus tell from such externals to what school a person learned in Torah belongs.

Against this background it is easy to see why the traditions collected by the rabbis include not only pronouncements but also stories.

III. ORAL TRANSMISSION

During the first four centuries of our era the verbalized Torah tradition of the Jewish rabbis grew enormously. And it was still being handed down orally. If one wonders how it was possible for such a huge body of text material to be preserved and passed on orally, one must consider the rabbis' pedagogical methods and the technique employed in oral transmission. I shall here provide a brief sketch of certain typical aspects of their oral instruction. The oldest specific evidence dates as a rule from the years following the fall of the temple (A.D. 70) and the destruction of Jerusalem (A.D. 135). But in essential aspects these methods are clearly ancient:

(1) I would emphasize first of all the fundamental role of *memorization*. We forget all too easily that this is a very old pedagogical

technique. Before the art of writing became common, memorization was the only way of preserving a statement or a text. And this primitive method proved to be very tenacious. Among Jewish teachers in antiquity we note that virtually all important knowledge was learned in the form of sayings and texts which were imprinted on the memory, so that one knew them by heart.[8] It must also be remembered that memorization is not some sophisticated academic specialty but rather a decidedly *popular* means of retaining articulated knowledge.

(2) A teaching pattern which shows up time after time is that of *text and commentary.* Methodical study is divided into two elements: (a) the learning of the text, and (b) the effort required to comprehend the meaning of the text: analysis, clarification, exposition. *Learning* a text and *understanding* it are, as we all know, two different matters, differing as memory does from intelligence. A written text must be produced before it can be commented upon. The same is true of oral tradition. First of all, an oral text must be, as it were, written on the student's memory; only then can the exegesis begin. The principle was: First learn, then understand.

(3) It is important that teachers speak tersely and incisively. They must avoid wordiness and vacuity in speech. If they wish to impress their wisdom upon the memories of their students, they must express themselves in concise terms. The rabbis used to say that one must always instruct in the briefest way possible (in Hebrew, *derek qesārāh*). For many centuries the teachers of wisdom in Israel cultivated the art of curbing their tongues. "Let your words be few," said the Preacher (Eccl 5:2), for example, and he was certainly thinking not only of prayer and conversation, but also of teaching. The rabbis kept up this tradition. "A sharp peppercorn is better than a basket full of cucumbers," they said. And the texts they have left behind are always extremely concentrated and terse.

(4) The teachers also made use of various *didactic and poetic devices.* For example, they used picturesque or pointed formulations,

---

[8] This method is by no means extinct in the Orient. Just recently a colleague—a Swedish professor of medicine—reported that he had lectured in Egypt. After his first lecture, a number of students came forward to ask if he could not summarize the major points of his presentation in such a way that they could be memorized. The mechanical memory has not been rejected in pedagogics all over the world!

alliteration, and assonance, rhythmic phrases, *parallelismus membrorum,* symmetrical arrangement of phrases, a verbatim repetition of introductory phrases, and so on. Such poetical devices were not of course utilized only to make statements easier to remember, but in practice they also served that purpose. It is easier to remember poetry than prose, rhythmic sentences than nonrhythmic, the picturesque than the pedestrian, the well-organized than the unorganized.

(5) *Repetition* is, in this context, self-evident and natural. The old Romans used to say that repetition is the mother of all knowledge. Ancient Jewish pedagogy was in complete agreement. The teachers would repeat their main points word by word, several times, and the students would then reiterate those same points over and over until they knew them by heart. Written texts were learned in the same manner: they were drilled into the students until they were memorized. Knowledge thus acquired was then retained by diligent, word-for-word repetition. In the rabbinical writings we often see a picture of the ideal scholar. He never sits idle in his house, but he sits there repeating and meditating. He never goes about absentminded or filled with worldly thoughts. He recites and meditates while he is going. The admonitions found in Deut 6:6–7 no doubt formed the ideal: "And these words which I command you this day shall be upon your heart; and you shall teach them diligently to your children, and shall talk of them when you sit in your house, and when you walk by the way, and when you lie down, and when you rise" (cf. also Josh 1:8 and Ps 1:1–2).

(6) When the texts were read and repeated, this was done not in an ordinary, conversational tone, but rhythmically and melodiously, as a *recitation.* The words were half sung, "cantillated." In antiquity reading was normally done aloud. The same held true for oral repetition. Only certain very sensitive secrets were whispered. Thus we see that in the transmission of the texts the very sound of the words and the rhythm and melody of the sentences play an interesting role.

(7) Many teachers and students also utilized the *art of writing* as an aid in the preservation of important instruction and tradition. Most of the Jewish teachers in the centuries from the birth of Christ and onward were able to write. But it is still hard to determine the role that writing may have played in their teaching and oral transmission. According to tradition, the Pharisaic-rabbinical movement

in Judaism maintained a distinction between written Torah and oral Torah, and deliberately propagated the view that oral Torah is to be handed down verbally and not in book form. But whether or not this principle was already recognized in Jesus' time is a subject of debate. The Jewish-American scholar Jacob Neusner published in 1971 a sizable work entitled *The Rabbinic Traditions about the Pharisees before 70.*[9] This is in many respects a most helpful study. Neusner here works through many of the same questions I dealt with in my dissertation *Memory and Manuscript.* I must of course lament the way he caricatures my positions. Neusner's work does, however, have its Achilles' heel. He has accepted as his main thesis an idea of his teacher Morton Smith, and sets out consciously to substantiate it.[10] Smith's thesis is that no real evidence enables us to determine the methods of transmission utilized in the early Christian congregations or by the Pharisees prior to A.D. 70. According to Smith and Neusner the memorizing technique we see used by the rabbis was a radical novelty, introduced by the rabbinical schools during the second century A.D. This novelty also included the rule that oral Torah was to be handed down verbally, with no help from (official) books. I am not at all convinced that Neusner is justified in reaching the final conclusion that we know nothing of how the Pharisees preserved their traditions prior to A.D. 70. After eliminating statements and evidence found in the rabbinical literature, in Josephus, and in the New Testament, Neusner can only assert that the rabbis introduced a radically new methodology after the fall of the temple and discuss why this occurred.[11]

I still maintain that the Pharisees and their scribes distinguished between written and oral Torah already in New Testament times, and that they did not accept any official books containing oral Torah. But—and this is the point here—this practice did not prevent their making *private notations* of material found in the oral tradition. In other words, a distinction was made between official

---

[9] 3 vols.; Leiden: Brill, 1971.

[10] See Smith's negative review of *Memory and Manuscript* in *Journal of Biblical Literature* 82 (1963): 169–76.

[11] [Later on Neusner changed his view; see his foreword to the new edition of *Memory and Manuscript* and *Tradition and Transmission* (1998), above n. 5.]

books and private memoranda. In the rabbinical tradition we can glimpse records of various kinds: "scrolls of secrets," notebooks, and other memoranda. Such probably appeared among the students of Hillel and Shammai as early as Jesus' time. Private notations of this kind were found above all in the schools of the Hellenistic world, where they were referred to as *hypomnēmata, apomnēmoneumata, chreiai,* and so on.

I would add parenthetically that we are still waiting for a solid dissertation which, on the basis of a careful investigation of written notes of this kind in the Hellenistic schools, would enable us to determine the role such memoranda played among Jesus' disciples and among the teachers and traditionists of the early church. In 1946 an all-too-brief but stimulating book dealing with such problems was published (posthumously). The author was the English provost R. O. P. Taylor, and the book was entitled *The Groundwork of the Gospels.*[12] This work has not received the attention it deserves. It should also be mentioned that in the past few years a clear tendency to emphasize strongly the role of *written* transmission in early Christianity has appeared, particularly among American scholars. Some even go so far as to deny that the Jesus tradition ever existed as a purely oral tradition. How far one can carry this train of thought is still an open question.[13]

(8) The rabbis did not appreciate studies limited to mere cramming and mechanical recitation. They were very conscious of the importance of comprehending and personally applying that which had been impressed upon one's mind. For this reason they carried on an energetic *struggle against lifeless knowledge.* They criticized with both humor and irony those who had memorized great masses of textual material without understanding what their own mouth was saying. They compared such persons to magicians who mumble formulas which they do not understand, or to lifeless baskets filled with scrolls. According to the rabbis a disciple ought not be a dead receptacle for the received tradition. He should rather enter into it so that

---

[12] Oxford: Blackwell, 1946.

[13] As a guide to this discussion I refer the reader to E. Earl Ellis, "New Directions in Form Criticism," *Jesus Christus in Historie und Theologie: Neutestamentl. Festschrift für Hans Conzelmann zum 60 Geburtstag* (ed. G. Strecker; Tübingen: Mohr [Siebeck], 1975), 299–315.

he understands it and is in agreement with it. Only thus can he actually live according to it, be a fruitful steward of it, and pass it on to others in an infectious way. A living bearer of the tradition is to be like a torch which has been lit by an older torch, in order that it might itself light others.

IV. ALLUSIONS TO THE TORAH TRADITION IN THE NEW TESTAMENT

In Acts 22:3 Luke has Paul speak as follows to a crowd in Jerusalem: "I am a Jew, born at Tarsus in Cilicia, but brought up in this city at the feet of Gamaliel, educated according to the strict manner of the law of our fathers, being zealous (a *zēlōtēs*) for God as you all are this day."

Luke's Paul here summarizes the comprehensive norm-system by which he has been brought up and educated within the Jewish community with the words: "the law of our fathers" *(ho patrōos nomos)*. This same Paul, in Acts 28:17, uses the comprehensive designation: "the customs of our fathers" *(ta ethē ta patrōa)*. It is also of interest to note that (in Acts 22:3, quoted above) he mentions by name his chief teacher, Gamaliel.

In Gal 1:14 Paul himself speaks of his youth: "I advanced in Judaism *(ioudaïsmos)* beyond many of my own age among my people, so extremely zealous was I for the traditions of my fathers *(hai patrikai mou paradoseis)*." With these words the apostle refers to the authoritative tradition which the leading teachers of the Jewish people in the New Testament times preserved and set forth.

The very same Jewish tradition is also mentioned in the Synoptic Gospels. Particularly helpful for our purposes here is the pericope dealing with mealtime customs in Mark 7 and Matthew 15. Here we see references to "the tradition of the elders" (Mark 7:3, 5; Matt 15:2), a tradition which "the Pharisees and all Jews" (Mark), "the scribes and the Pharisees" (Matthew) uphold in addition to "God's commandments" in the sacred scriptures. Other terms from the Jewish tradition of a technical or quasi-technical nature also appear: "to pass on" (as tradition, *paradidonai*, Mark 7:13); "to receive" (as tradition, *paralambanein*, Mark 7:4); "to keep" the tradition (*tērein*, Mark 7:9); "to maintain" the tradition (*kratein*, Mark 7:3, 8); "to uphold" the tradition (*histanai*, Mark 7:9 var.); "to walk according to" the tradition (*peripatein kata*, Mark 7:5); "to transgress" the tradition (*parabainein*, Matt 15:2).

Thus Paul and the evangelists are conscious of the fact that the Jews of their time have a tradition—consisting of many traditions—which they scrupulously maintain. The phrases they use indicate that this tradition is not accepted by all of the people, but also that it is of concern for others besides Pharisees. It is referred to as "the tradition of the fathers" or "the tradition of the elders," and the Pharisees and their scribes are understood to be its most influential representatives. The Jewish historian Josephus also indicates that the Pharisees had a dominant position among the people at that time.

V. TRADITION IN EARLY CHRISTIANITY

If we bear in mind that Paul of Tarsus was reared in this Jewish tradition, as it was upheld and observed and handed down by the Pharisaic scribes, it is of real interest to proceed to the writings of this same Paul as a Christian apostle. In these writings he speaks of the early church's own tradition. It will be worth our while to take note of the manner in which he speaks of this.[14]

According to Paul, the church possesses a normative standard which he refers to as "tradition" or "traditions" (*paradosis, paradoseis*, 1 Cor 11:2; 2 Thess 2:15; 3:6). The manner in which this is passed on is expressed in the verbs *paradidonai*, "hand over [tradition]" , and *paralambanein*, "receive [as tradition]", 1 Cor 11:23; 15:1, 3; Gal 1:9; Phil 4:9; 1 Thess 2:13; 4:1; 2 Thess 3:6. The young Christian congregations are to "maintain" or "hold fast to," or "uphold" these traditions; the verbs used here are, among others, *kratein* (2 Thess 2:15), *katechein* (1 Cor 11:2), and *hestēkenai* (1 Cor 15:1). We also have the expression "to walk according to" these traditions (*peripatein kata*, 2 Thess 3:6). In the deuteropauline Pastoral Epistles we find such

---

[14] See Oscar Cullmann, *Die Tradition als exegetisches, historisches und theologisches Problem* (Zürich: Zwingli-Verlag, 1954), 12–16; ET *The Early Church* (trans. A. J. B. Higgins and S. Godman; London: SCM Press, 1956), 63–66.

terms as *tērein* and *phylassein,* which mean "to keep," "to observe," "to hold" (1 Tim 5:21, 6:14, 20; 2 Tim 1:14).

On the basis of terminological agreement of this nature it is of course not possible to draw the simple conclusion that early Christianity possessed a tradition of precisely the same kind as did the Jews. Early Christianity was, as we well know, critical of the Jewish tradition and revolted against it. But we are entitled to establish one thing: in Paul's time early Christianity is conscious of the fact that it has *a tradition* of its own—including many traditions—which the church leaders hand on to the congregations, which the congregations receive, and which they then are to guard and live by. In Paul's time there exists a *conscious, deliberate, and programmatic* transmission in the early church.

One observation ought perhaps to be included here. The pioneers in the form-critical school were of the opinion that the early church, in its very first phase of development, was not disposed to pass on a tradition: it lacked that perspective on the future which is necessary if one is to see any reason for doing so. This indicates that the form-critical school had a one-sided understanding of transmission as taking place only from one generation to the next. In both the Jewish and the early Christian sources, however, we can see that tradition happens not only between generations but also within one and the same generation when binding material is passed on. Whenever authoritative material is passed on to someone who receives it, a form of transmission has taken place.

VI. PAUL AS A BEARER OF TRADITION

In several places in his letters, Paul tells us that he has passed on and that he passes on tradition—Christian tradition—to his congregations. What kind of a picture do we see in the Pauline Epistles of the apostle functioning in this role?

We who belong to the Lutheran branch of the Christian church ought—if any—to be conscious of how radically and spiritedly Paul speaks about freedom "in Christ," about the church's freedom, about the freedom of the individual Christian. For those who have been added to the body of Christ through baptism, all things are free, everything is permitted, all is pure. Everything belongs to them.

Their conduct of life is and must be a "walk in the Spirit." And "where the Spirit of the Lord is, there is freedom" (2 Cor 3:17). Paul is therefore the last one to want to place upon his congregations some kind of "yoke of bondage," an obligatory system of norms complete with commandments and decrees and rules.

It is precisely because he held such a view that it is of so great interest to note how Paul nevertheless speaks of the existence of a normative tradition and normative traditions within the church. Here a brief reminder of how Paul describes himself in his role as a bearer of tradition will suffice.

Paul looks upon himself as a spiritual father to those who have been won for the gospel (1 Cor 4:17; Phlm 10), and the congregations he has founded (1 Cor 4:14–17; 2 Cor 12:14; Gal 4:19; 1 Thess 2:11). And he admonishes his congregations to be imitators *(mimētai)* of him in all respects, even as he himself is an imitator of Christ (1 Cor 4:16; 11:1; 1 Thess 1:6; 2 Thess 3:7).

What the apostle has in mind when he speaks of imitating Christ and imitating Paul is naturally in the final analysis a great mystery, a fruit-bearing unity in the Spirit between the heavenly Lord and his true followers in the world. But Paul also thinks quite concretely of the life of imitation which comes into being when obedient disciples receive, and pattern their lives according to, the instruction of their teacher. We note for example that the admonition in 1 Cor 4:16, "Be imitators of me," is followed immediately by the concrete statement: "Therefore I sent to you Timothy, my beloved and faithful child in the Lord, to remind you of my ways in Christ, as I teach them everywhere in every church" (1 Cor 4:17). When Paul speaks of "my ways" he is referring to patterns of his life and teachings. *Imitatio Pauli* (imitating Paul) means, in large measure, the same as to receive and live according to the teaching which Paul proclaimed in all of his congregations. This involves, in the first place, instruction in words, both orally and in writing. In 2 Thess 2:15 the apostle writes to the congregation in Thessalonica: "So then, brethren, stand firm and hold to the traditions which you were taught by us, either by word of mouth or by letter." In Phil 4:9 we note further that Paul does not think only of the tradition which he passes on in articulated form—as words, spoken or written—but also of what he does and arranges. He says: "What you have learned and received [from me] and heard and seen in me, do." That tradition is not meant only for the individual can be seen in such passages as Phil 3:17: "Brethren, join in imitating me, and mark those who so live as you have an example in us."

These texts should be commented upon from various points of view, but I shall content myself with three observations: (1) The pneumatic, charismatic character of early Christianity does not exclude authoritative tradition and a conscious transmission. Even though Paul radically espouses the freedom of the Christian to "walk in the Spirit" before God, he nonetheless deliberately passes on tradition and traditions to his congregations, and requests them to accept them and live according to them.

(2) It is clear in Paul that the traditions are not intended only for individuals, but that they are given to the congregations to be upheld within the context of the Christian fellowship. The traditions belong to the common life of the early Christian communities. To this extent the assumptions of the form-critical school are supported by the material. But the fact is that Paul does not speak of the traditions as though they are the wind of the Spirit, or profound driving forces or tendencies which work anonymously in the congregations, spreading wildly from place to place. The transmission of tradition is first of all associated with the work of authoritative leaders of various kinds. The example provided in 1 Cor 4:16–17 is particularly clear. The normative tradition has come to the congregation directly from Paul, and it is brought to completion by Paul's disciple, Timothy—the apostle's spiritual son—who comes to the congregation in order to instruct them further concerning the "ways," that is, the teachings and the way of life which Paul customarily impresses on all of his congregations.

(3) We must also note that the tradition has different dimensions. The fact that Paul passes on tradition—and traditions—to his congregations means that he imparts to them a faith, a spirit, a confession, a proclamation, an instruction with an inner power scarcely accessible for analysis, but which nonetheless took place through *external forms,* of which we can catch a glimpse behind his descriptions. We can see most clearly the *verbal* dimension of the tradition he provided (oral and written), and quite clearly too of the *practical* dimension (a model way of life, a model pattern for

"how you ought to live and to please God," words taken from another passage, 1 Thess 4:1). But we also sense here the *institutional* dimension of the Pauline tradition: forms of organization that will enable the believers to function as a congregation (e.g., 1 Cor 11:34b; 14:26–40).

VII. PAUL AND THE JESUS TRADITION

Now we shall pose the next question: In the diversified tradition which he passed on to his congregations, did Paul also include traditions about Jesus, what he had said and done during his earthly life? In other words, did Paul include that which we customarily refer to as gospel tradition or Jesus tradition?

Many scholars are of the opinion that Paul neither wanted to know anything about Jesus' earthly activity nor actually knew anything significant about it. For a number of exegetes this is such an obvious fact and so cherished a belief that they can only smile at any attempt to ascertain what Paul could have known of Jesus' words and deeds. I find this an amazing position.

It is certain that Paul does not quote the earthly Jesus very often in his epistles, nor does he discuss such material. But neither are his epistles entirely free of direct quotations from the Jesus tradition. Furthermore, he repeats in his epistles time after time that he already has handed down an authoritative tradition to his congregations (e.g., 1 Cor 11:2, 23; 15:1–3; Gal 1:9; Phil 4:9; 1 Thess 2:13; 4:1; 2 Thess 2:15; 3:6), and he makes references to that which his hearers have already heard or already have knowledge of (e.g., Phil 4:9; 1 Thess 2:13; 2 Thess 2:15). We further note that Paul often develops his argumentation on the basis of certain premises which he assumes are shared by his readers. It seems to me to be a highly legitimate historical task to attempt to answer such questions as these: What was the nature of the authoritative tradition material which Paul had passed on to his congregations before he wrote his epistles to them? And did this material include gospel tradition?

Time does not permit us to discuss here the entire question concerning the extent of Paul's knowledge of the Jesus tradition as revealed in his epistles, how much he takes for granted and hints at in his presentations. I shall be content to touch briefly upon a few

passages in which he clearly *adduces* Jesus tradition, and two passages
where he *quotes* directly.

The apostle writes in 1 Cor 7:10: "To the married I give charge,
not I but the Lord, that the wife should not separate from her hus-
band." In verse 12 he continues as follows: "To the rest I say, not the
Lord, that if any brother has a wife who is an unbeliever, and she
consents to live with him, he should not divorce her." And further
on (in v. 25) he asserts: "Now concerning the unmarried, I have no
command of the Lord, but I give my opinion as one who by the
Lord's mercy is trustworthy." Here Paul is providing instruction in a
context of *halakah;* he is providing authoritative guidance for the
Christian congregation in questions regarding marriage. And in the
process of doing so he makes reference to the words of Jesus (cf. Matt
5:32; 19:9). He does not quote word for word but expresses the *intent*
of the words while he himself formulates the terse regulations. We
also note that Paul—in the manner of a rabbi—clearly indicates the
authority which stands behind the rules in question. He makes a
clear distinction between his own words and those of the Lord.

Finally, we observe how Paul proceeds when he does not have a
specific word from Jesus to support him. He then states without cir-
cumlocution that in such cases he cannot refer to any command of
the Lord, but is simply providing his own opinion. These passages
are embarrassing evidence against the common opinion that in the
early church no distinction was made between what was said "by the
Lord [himself]" and what was said by some one else "in the Lord";
that words of Jesus were freely constructed, or that sayings of some
early Christian prophet were freely placed in the mouth of Jesus. In
1 Corinthians 7 we see how such a man as Paul, at least on occasion,
very clearly upheld the distinction between that which was said "by
the Lord" and that which was said "in the Lord."

In 1 Cor 9:14 the apostle writes: "In the same way, the Lord
commanded that those who proclaim the gospel should get their living by the gospel." In this passage Paul does not quote the words of
Jesus, but himself formulates a halakah-type statement that one may
draw from them (cf. Matt 10:9–10; Luke 10:7). Here Paul presup-
poses the words of Jesus.

Another instance in which Paul appears to be referring to a saying of Jesus is found in 1 Thess 4:15. The question here touched upon

is not halakic, but eschatological or apocalyptic. Paul writes: "For this we declare to you by the word of the Lord *(en logō Kyriou),* that we who are alive, who are left until the coming of the Lord, shall not precede those who have fallen asleep." It seems probable here that Paul is referring directly to a transmitted saying of Jesus. But he does not quote this saying directly in this instance either; he is simply expressing in his own words the answer which he has extracted from the saying of Jesus regarding this question.

We must now leave such texts and turn to the two passages in which Paul expressly *quotes* gospel tradition. These are found in 1 Cor 11:23–25; and 15:1–8. In both instances the text which has been handed down is introduced with a formula indicating that the apostle is quoting directly. 1 Cor 11:23 begins as follows: "For I received *(paralambanein)* from the Lord what I also delivered *(paradidonai)* to you, that . . . ." In 15:3 we read: "For I delivered to you first of all what I also received, how that . . . ."

The tradition text quoted by the apostle in the first instance (1 Cor 11:23–25) is the account of Jesus' Last Supper. The wording is not Paul's but is traditional. The version quoted is the one which (in a later form) was also written down by Luke (22:19–20; cf. the parallels). If we scrutinize the apostle's line of thought, we note that he is here concerned to build upon the actual words of Jesus in the text, that the bread is "my body" and the cup is "the new covenant in my blood." This is undoubtedly the reason why Paul says that he has received this from the Lord *(apo tou Kyriou).* The idea is then that the Lord spoke these words to the disciples who were present on the occasion of the Last Supper, and that these men subsequently passed the tradition on.

The other tradition text (1 Cor 15:3–8) includes a brief summary of the decisive events in the Jesus' story: "that Christ died for our sins in accordance with the scriptures, that he was buried, that he is raised on the third day in accordance with the scriptures, and that he appeared to Cephas, then to the twelve," and so on. Paul does not here name the person who passed this text on to him; he simply says that he received it as tradition. But we note both in the quotation formula and in the non-Pauline wording employed in the quoted text that he is repeating a traditional text.

It is clear from these passages that Paul is aware of a way of handing on the Jesus tradition in the form of direct quotation; in other words, he knows how to transmit a text which has been formulated in a fixed manner. And if we ask ourselves what this old rabbinical student has in mind when he says that he has "delivered" to the congregation words which he himself has "received," it seems that we have merely two possibilities to choose between. Either the apostle has passed the text on in a written form which the congregation then has at its disposal, or he has presented the text orally, and impressed it upon them in such a way that the congregation (or more precisely, one or more of its leaders) knows it by heart. To "hand over" a text is not the same as to recite it once. It rather means that the text is presented to the hearers in such a way that they have "received" it and possess it. For my own part I find it easiest to assume that Paul is referring here to an *oral* transmission.

By drawing on a number of Pauline texts, I have pointed out that the apostle obviously was well acquainted with a variety of ways of transmitting tradition. The two passages we have just considered (1 Cor 11:23–25 and 15:1–8) reveal to us (I can interpret this in no other way) that Paul also was familiar with and utilized a simple, direct *transmitting of texts,* when that was necessary; that is, he quite simply passed on a text to a recipient, either in writing or orally. In the latter case the text was *taught* to the recipient in such a way that he knew it by heart. It was written upon his mind. This was a delimited activity in itself, not a component part of an ongoing process of proclamation or instruction.

Perhaps I should mention how I came upon this idea. It happened in the year 1955/1956 when I was occupied with a licentiate dissertation on the Epistle of James. As is well known, Martin Dibelius has written the most influential commentary on this epistle.[15] In his opinion, James is a typical product of early Christian parenesis (exhortation). Dibelius believes that the sayings of Jesus in the synoptic tradition had their primary *Sitz im Leben* in early Christian parenesis; it was there that they were passed on. The Epistle of James is full of allusions to the sayings of Jesus, most of these from the Sermon on the Mount. But as I studied these allusions, it came to me that the words

---

[15] *Brief des Jakobus* (KEK 15; Göttingen: Vandenhoeck & Ruprecht, 1921); ET *A Commentary on the Epistle of James* (revised by H. Greeven; trans. M. A. Williams; Hermeneia; Philadelphia: Fortress, 1976).

of Jesus in the Synoptic Gospels cannot have had their primary *Sitz im Leben* in early Christian parenesis. It seems completely clear that those involved in parenesis were not inclined to make quotations. The exhortations are generally delivered in a traditional manner; they are full of borrowed motifs, ideas, words, and phrases. They reflect little originality on the part of the speaker. But those who admonish intend to do so themselves, on their own authority, and not to quote others. We even find that quotations from the sacred scriptures are few and far between in parenesis. The scriptures are alluded to, motifs and formulations are derived from them, but they are almost never quoted. The same is true of the relationship of parenesis to the oral tradition. In parenesis speakers use a traditional style, borrowing raw material; but they do the speaking themselves; they do not quote. They do not intend to pass on specific words received from others. For this reason the Sermon on the Mount and the Epistle of James do not come from the same *Sitz im Leben*. Similarly, the tractate *Pirke Avot* (The sayings of the fathers) does not come from the same *Sitz im Leben* as the parenetic parts of Jewish literature. There is a distinct difference between collections of traditional sayings and the like, and parenetic admonition. They constitute two different forms *(Gattungen)* for presenting material.

Dibelius is, in part, quite clear about this. He takes the position that early Christianity handed down the sayings of Jesus in two ways: in parenetic contexts, and in collections which contained exclusively sayings of Jesus, which the missionaries took with them either in oral or written form.[16] But for Dibelius, the former way was the primary one. For my part, I cannot see how parenesis has any claim at all to be the basic *Sitz im Leben* for the words of Jesus. The Jesus traditions were a part of the traditional material which one merely *built upon* and *alluded to* in parenesis.

I suspect, on the other hand, that Paul has provided us with a dependable clue by quoting in two passages texts which he expressly designates as verbal tradition. Here we sense the primary *Sitz im Leben* for the early Christian transmission of Jesus tradition; this is, paradoxical though it may seem, transmission itself, transmission as a conscious, technical act of instruction.

---

[16] *From Tradition to Gospel* (n. 1), 242.

Before leaving this theme I must make a number of observations:

(1) In 1 Cor 11:23–25 and 15:1–8 Paul is not specifically *handing down* the two texts which he quotes. He is not providing new Jesus traditions for the congregation. He is simply repeating two traditions which he explicitly says he already has delivered to the congregation. If we suppose that the congregation in Corinth had understood and held fast to the instruction Paul had previously provided concerning the Lord's Supper and his death and resurrection, then Paul really would have had no reason to repeat these two traditions in his letter; he had already passed them on to the congregation. In that case we would have known even less about what he delivered to his congregations prior to writing to them. That is worth thinking about.

(2) In spite of the fact that Paul repeats traditional texts which he has received from others, he feels free to insert interpretive elements into them, to make certain additions to transmitted texts. The parenthetical remark that Paul makes in 1 Cor 15:6 ("most of whom are still alive, though some have fallen asleep") is certainly an addition which the apostle makes to the text he has received. Then too, we cannot be certain where his direct quotation in 1 Cor 15:3–8 ends. This may be because the apostle in this instance does not intend to pass on a traditional text in authentic form for the first time to his readers, but simply repeats a text which the congregation has already received in its basic form. But I doubt that this explanation is the whole story. We see in the Synoptic Gospels that the Jesus tradition has been reworked during the period of its transmission in the early church, that abridgments and additions have been made in an effort to make the meaning clearer. So it is not without interest to note that here in 1 Corinthians 15 Paul has made certain small interpretive alterations of the text. We shall return to this later on.

(3) The text which Paul repeats in 1 Corinthians 15 is a particularly significant one, for this is a summary of the basic kerygma, listing the decisive events connected with the death and resurrection of Jesus. But even so, not all of the traditions which he points to here by using brief association-words (e.g., "he appeared to Cephas, then to the twelve") have been preserved in the Synoptic Gospels. Particularly amazing is the loss of the tradition concerning the appearance of the resurrected Jesus to Cephas, the fundamental, first appearance

of the resurrected One (unless a fragment of this has been preserved in Matt 16:18–19). Also without a trace are the traditions about the appearance of the resurrected Jesus to more than five hundred brethren at one time, and the appearance to James. This omission serves as a reminder that we cannot simply equate the Jesus traditions passed on by Paul to his congregations at their inception with any one of our Synoptic Gospels, or all three together. It will not do therefore, to think of our gospels as copies of a complete and mechanically unaltered recording of Jesus' teaching and of the first-hand reports of eyewitnesses.

VIII. EARLY CHRISTIANITY AND THE PAST

The apostles, evangelists, and teachers of early Christianity wanted to address the people of their day, to speak to their listeners about something of concern to them. Naturally they were not concerned to provide documentation and archives for dead memories from the past. I can go along with Martin Dibelius to this extent, when he elegantly describes how early Christianity lived in the present and in an intensively longed-for future.

But the whole argument is distorted if one forgets that early Christianity nonetheless had a genuine interest in the past and a natural feeling for the fact that ancestors and earlier generations no longer live here on earth, as well as for the fact that God's activities have their appointed times, inexorably following one after the other. Furthermore, early Christianity had a special reason for being interested in one specific aspect of the past: the past as it concerned Jesus of Nazareth, who, after a remarkable ministry, was crucified by Pontius Pilate, and then arose from the dead.

None of the evangelists intends to write about a dead man's final destiny. All of them write about a person whom they understand to be alive today, a celestial Lord to whom they daily turn in prayer and other acts of worship. But they write about his work in Israel during an era which lies in the past. It is not true to say that they give free, concrete expression to their present faith in the heavenly Lord, and to their answers "in Christ's Spirit" to contemporary questions, by creating myths about what he says to the congregations today. Not even John, whose desire to permit Jesus' divine splendor to shine through in his words and deeds has strongly influenced the style of the Fourth Gospel, writes simply about the present for the present. He is conscious of a chronological, spatial, and factual distance between himself and Jesus' activity in Galilee and Judea. He writes of a time when "the Spirit had not yet been given," "when Jesus was not yet glorified," when Jesus had not yet been "lifted up from the earth" so that he might "draw all people [even the pagan Gentiles] to himself," a time when the disciples "did not yet understand," inasmuch as the Spirit of truth had not yet come to "guide them into all truth"—to use some of John's own formulations (7:39; 12:16, 32; 16:13; cf. also 2:22).

We see in the Synoptics even more clearly than in John how the evangelists and their sources look back to an era which lies in the past and is separated from the present not only chronologically but also spatially and factually. It is admittedly true that this perspective has been broken through or toned down in various places—the splendor of the resurrection has colored the traditions—but this in no way detracts from the general impression that the intent of the evangelists is to describe the ministry of Jesus in Israel up to and including his death and resurrection in Jerusalem. It is a ministry which leads forward to the exalted position Jesus has in the present, but this goal is not reached until the final chapter.

For my part, I find the way Jesus' closest followers are described in the Gospels well worth considering. When the evangelists write, Peter, James, and John—indeed, all of the Twelve—are men of reputation in the church. They are spoken of with reverence, and their spirit and power are the subject of stories. In Acts 5:15 Luke reports a popular legend about Peter that he could heal sick people merely by passing by them so that his shadow fell upon them. That is indicative of the high opinion people had of Peter when the evangelists wrote. But when the evangelists come to write about Jesus' earthly activity in Galilee and Jerusalem, Peter and James and John and the other disciples are presented not as a group of spiritual heroes, but as men conspicuously weak and immature, lacking in knowledge and understanding. This is not the situation in the church after Easter but the situation during Jesus' earthly ministry. It does show that the early Christians preserved memories of the past, and sensed the distance between themselves and the past. There is a tendency in the tradition as time went on—we see it in Matthew, Luke, and John—to tone down the negative presentation of Jesus' closest disciples in the older texts; but this tendency merely confirms our observation. Herbert Braun says in his book *Jesus*[17] that there is also a tendency in the gospel tradition to depict the disciples as worse and worse, but he provides no evidence of this tendency, nor can it be proved.

This characteristic looking backward in time is found in the Gospels, but is it perhaps not found in the tradition's oldest form? Could it be that we are dealing with a secondary historicizing? Jürgen Roloff has posed this question in his book *Das Kerygma und der irdische Jesus,*[18] and he demonstrates that this was not the case. Even in the layers which are usually looked upon as the oldest, we can see that early Christians were conscious of the distance between themselves and Jesus' earthly ministry. Roloff provides a number of examples which indicate that the situation as described in the gospel tradition does not at all reflect the circumstances in the church after Easter, and he shows that Jesus' activity prior to the crucifixion is described in the gospel tradition as a veiled appearance, limited in space, without success, and tied to conditions which presuppose his time and situation. The early church has tried to understand these past events better, has interpreted them, has even permitted its interpretations to affect the material. But the early Christians preserved the memory of a distinct segment of past history and felt their dependence on it. Thus the problems of the young Christian congregations have *colored* the material, but not *created* it. This looking back upon Jesus' earthly ministry is an essential factor in early Christian tradition formation right from the very beginning.

IX. THE CONCENTRATION ON "THE ONLY TEACHER"

The primary characteristic of all of the books in the New Testament is undoubtedly the central role played in them by the person of

---

[17] *Jesus: Der Mann aus Nazareth und seine Zeit* (Themen der Theologie 1; Stuttgart: Kreuz-Verlag, 1969), 48; ET *Jesus of Nazareth: The Man and His Time* (trans. Everett R. Kalin; Philadelphia: Fortress, 1979).

[18] *Das Kerygma und der irdische Jesus: Historische Motive in den Jesus-Erzählungen der Evangelien* (Göttingen: Vandenhoeck & Ruprecht, 1970).

Jesus Christ. This is especially obvious in the four gospels. They were written exclusively in order to present Jesus. Other people of course appear in them too: Jesus has his followers; he soon has his bitter opponents; the masses respond to his activity, first receptively, only to turn against him at the end. The disciples, the opponents, and the masses all play distinctive roles, which the evangelists describe with consistency. But the spotlight is always on Jesus. The purpose of the Gospels is to describe him and no one else: *his* appearance in Israel, what *he* said, what *he* did, what happened to *him*. It is true that there are traditions which deal with John the Baptist, but this is the case simply because his fate becomes intertwined with that of Jesus.

It is worthy of notice that the evangelists give Jesus' closest disciples quite insignificant roles in what happens; I have already touched on this. During the decades between the departure of Jesus and the appearance of the Gospels, men such as Peter and James and John certainly said many things that might have been considered worthy of being recorded and given to the congregations. But never for a moment do the evangelists yield to the temptation to supplement what Jesus has to say with a speech of Peter or James or John. Their intention is to present Jesus and no one else.

Matthew quotes Jesus as saying: "For you have [only] one teacher *(didaskalos)* and you are all brethren" (23:8). This saying is presumably secondary (an interpretation), but it nevertheless gives expression to an attitude which all four of the evangelists seem to have shared. They are concerned exclusively with what Jesus has said to God's congregation (and done for it). I shall return later to the question of how those with such a concern nonetheless seem to feel free to rework the tradition and to reformulate some of the sayings of Jesus.

The extraordinary concentration upon Jesus becomes particularly obvious when the Gospels are compared with the literature of Jewish tradition. Many teachers appear in the latter; the Talmud refers to nearly two thousand rabbis by name. They are all held in esteem, they are quoted with respect. But here interest is centered on Torah, not on any individual rabbi. Statements made by different rabbis are placed side by side; the authority of one differs from that of another only by degree. That is not the case in the Gospels. One figure—Jesus—stands in a class by himself, enjoying a unique authority. Whenever he appears, he dominates the scene in a sovereign manner. No one even approaches his stature.

If one thinks about this, it becomes extremely difficult to imagine that there ever was a time when Jesus' followers were not interested in preserving his teachings and in committing his deeds to memory. And if we orient ourselves historically, and remind ourselves how students in the Jewish milieu hung on the words of their teachers and attentively followed their activities in order to learn how to live properly, it then becomes difficult to believe that Jesus' disciples could have been less concerned to hear their master, to observe his way of doing things, and to store up all of this in their memories.

As the Gospels also reveal, this concentration upon Jesus in regard to content is matched by a formal concentration upon Jesus. The evangelists are conscious theologians; this is clear from the way they design their work, group their material, form connecting notices, omit formulations, add formulations, alter formulations. But they do not see it as their task to write a reasoned presentation of Jesus, setting forth his message and doctrines in their own words mixed in with theological comments, doctrinal argumentation, or hortatory statements. They permit Jesus to speak for himself, as a rule in direct discourse. They report episodes involving Jesus tersely and to the point. They do not allow themselves to comment— except for occasional, concise, and scarcely noticeable remarks in links between pericopes. This is very conspicuous when the Gospels are compared to the other books in the New Testament. We shall return to this later.[19]

X. CONTINUITY IN THE VIEW OF JESUS

This concentration upon Jesus—the *isolation* of the Jesus tradition—has not escaped the attention of Rudolf Bultmann. With a

---

[19] [On the theme of this section see now above all Samuel Byrskog, *Jesus the Only Teacher: Didactic Authority and Transmission in Ancient Judaism and the Matthean Community* (ConBNT 24; Stockholm: Almqvist & Wiksell International, 1994).]

reference to Gerhard Kittel, he emphasizes this prominent characteristic in the early Christian collections of gospel traditions.[20] But
according to Bultmann, the first evangelist (Mark) is so far removed
from the earthly Jesus that he can only hear the whisper of his voice.
Two wide and deep chasms separate Mark from the Jesus who was
crucified by Pontius Pilate: that between Jesus and the original Palestinian community after Easter, and that between this early Palestinian Christianity and early Hellenistic Christianity.

Bultmann contends that Jesus' activity was entirely non-
messianic. To the extent that material in the traditions show characteristics which may be classified as messianic, it must be judged as
secondary. The conditions necessary for the rise of the Jesus tradition did not exist until after Easter. It is true that many Jesus traditions appear in the early Palestinian community: people remembered
him, gathered information, even added Jesus traditions of their own
making. Collections of such traditions also began to appear. But
these collections were merely "enumerations and summings up"
(Aufreihungen, Summierungen). Early Palestinian Christianity lacked
the dominant concept around which the Jesus traditions could be
organized into a coherent unity: the myth about the crucified and
risen Lord. This myth had its origins in the Hellenistic community
and was given form in the Hellenistic church's basic message
(kērygma). Thus Mark was able to produce the first coherent gospel:
he used this myth and this kerygma as his point of departure.

It is difficult today to go along with Bultmann's train of
thought. And it just is not true that it is based simply upon a detailed
analysis of the traditional gospel material, free of all presuppositions.
On the contrary, this train of thought is also built upon a priori
presuppositions:

(1) When one labels all of the so-called messianic characteristics
in the gospel traditions secondary, that judgment is based in large
measure on the view one has of what Jesus was like and of what the
earliest Christian kerygma amounted to.

(2) When it is asserted that tradition formation could have
begun only after Easter, that is based not least of all on the manner in
which one envisions a tradition-building community. Heinz Schürmann

---

[20] Rudolf Bultmann, *History* (n. 2), 368–69.

has shown in a famous essay that the sociological conditions required for the appearance of gospel tradition must have been present already in the community which gathered around the earthly Jesus.[21]

(3) When one makes a clear distinction between Palestinian and Hellenistic Christianity, one is building upon a clear-cut distinction between "Palestinian" and "Hellenistic" which is no longer tenable. We now know that Hellenistic culture had gained a secure footing on Palestinian soil even before Jesus' time—even among the Aramaic-speaking Jews.

These are complicated questions, but I am going to attempt to describe my primary objection very briefly. I contend that the material shows an obvious continuity in the Jesus tradition, a continuity revealed not least at its very heart, in the view of Jesus.

In those layers of the gospel tradition which are generally considered the oldest, Jesus already appears with an overwhelming authority *(exousia)*. He preaches and teaches about the reign of God; he heals sick people and expels demons in a remarkable manner. It is also typical that he concentrates on rescuing the socially and religiously downtrodden. Jesus does not say much about himself, but he conducts himself with supreme authority, and his disciples treat him with unreserved veneration and devotion. The amazement of the masses is a part of this picture too. In my judgment, a rather straight line proceeds from this situation to the situation after Easter, when early Christianity worships Jesus as the Messiah, God's Son, the Lord *(Kyrios)*. A development has taken place—a many-sided, complicated development—above all because of what has happened to Jesus, but also because the faith of his followers has been strengthened and developed. But a fundamental continuity may be seen in the exclusive and dominant position Jesus occupies in the eyes of his disciples. In an engrossing study entitled *The Mission and Achievement of Jesus*,[22] Reginald H. Fuller has put it that the "raw material"

---

[21] Heinz Schürmann, "Die vorösterlichen Anfänge der Logientradition," in *Der historische Jesus und der kerygmatische Christus* (ed. H. Ristow and K. Matthiai; 2d ed.; Berlin: Evangelische Verlagsanstalt, 1961), 342–70. Reprinted in *Traditionsgeschichtliche Untersuchungen zu den synoptischen Evangelien* (KBANT; Düsseldorf: Patmos-Verlag, 1968), 37–65.

[22] SBT 12; London: SCM Press, 1954.

for the high Christology of the early church is already present in the traditions from Jesus' earthly ministry. That, I believe, is a quite appropriate way of describing the situation.

Let me discuss three examples: (1) From what we know of the use of titles in Palestine at the beginning of our era, we have every reason to believe that from the very first day of his public manifestation in Israel Jesus was addressed as "Lord" ("my Lord," "our Lord"; in Aramaic, *māri, māran,* or *māranā;* in Greek, *Kyrie).* It was thus that honored persons were addressed. It seems that this title has remained a part of the Jesus tradition all the way, only gaining in potency, steadily acquiring greater weight and significance. The title was appropriate the whole time, while Jesus' authoritative teaching and mighty deeds elevated him in the eyes of his followers and at last placed him at the right hand of power as "King of kings and Lord of lords," with a name that coincides with "the name that is above all other names." This development was advanced significantly by the Easter event, with the certainty that Jesus had been exalted after his suffering. But it would be hard to prove that a radically new trend began at that point, and even harder to say that this new trend appeared first of all in the Hellenistic branch of early Christianity. I do not believe that the title Lord *(Kyrios)* can be used to demonstrate that there was a break in the development of the Jesus tradition.

(2) A similar continuity can be seen in the Son of God title. The idea that Israel is God's son was cherished in the Old Testament and in the later Jewish tradition, and the king of Israel is called God's son, for example, in the Psalter (2:7). In the fragmentary midrash to 2 Samuel 7 found at Qumran (4QFlor 1:10–13), we note that this title could be used in reference to the coming Messiah as well. And in the intertestamental literature (Sirach, the Wisdom of Solomon) as in the rabbinical writings, we have evidence that this idea could be democratized and individualized and used to refer to righteous individuals in Israel. In the New Testament material we find that the young church after Easter designates Jesus as God's Son in a special sense; he stands over all others and has a unique right to call God his Father. Old formulations—for example, in Rom 1:3—reveal to us that the early Christian view of Jesus as God's Son received new dimensions in and through the appearance of resurrection faith. But how can we say with any historical justification that Jesus' disciples

had not already regarded him as God's Son in a special sense? Throughout the entire synoptic tradition it is striking how intimately Jesus speaks to God and about God. It seems to me that Joachim Jeremias is too bold when he asserts that in the Jewish milieu of Jesus' time it was unthinkable to address God as Abba (Father). Our source material related to the way contemporary Jewish groups addressed God in prayer is too limited to enable us to say with certainty what was *not* done. But the impression derived from the gospel tradition of Jesus' unaffected but close intimacy with God the Father remains, expressed most clearly in his use of the prayer-address *Abba.* Thus we can recognize a continuity and development in the Son of God Christology comparable to that with the title Lord.

(3) With regard to Jesus' attitude toward the title Messiah/Christ, I find it hard to avoid the impression that the contemporary discussion often suffers from a certain anachronism in the very way in which the problem is posed. We carry on our debate as though this title was already extant with its specifically Christian significance before Jesus appeared, and as though the point in question is this: Did Jesus want to be Messiah in this sense or not? In reality the fully formed Messiah Christology of the early church was the result of a development which gave the title a rather specific content. Before Jesus came, the term *Messiah* simply did not have the meaning we attach to it.

From the historical point of view the question should be whether Jesus wanted to be Messiah in the sense in which the term was commonly used among the Jews at the beginning of our era: whether he desired to be the liberator who would deliver the people of Israel from their enemies and oppressors and secure for them political freedom (even hegemony) in addition to all spiritual blessings. It seems clear that Jesus rejected the title understood in that sense. It is another question how Jesus thought of himself and his mission, with its peculiar relation with the coming reign of God, and whether he permitted his disciples to use the Messiah title as a designation of him in this mission. These are more difficult questions, but they are of interest: in the gospel tradition we see how Jesus corrects his disciples' picture of his own life's course as well as theirs by teaching them the necessity of humbling oneself and sacrificing oneself in accordance with the will of God. The ideal picture of Jesus, which in the course of time takes form, is given the Messiah title, and this title becomes so important that it serves as Jesus' second name. But the fact is that the significance which the early church gave this title was in large measure modeled on the picture it had of *Jesus* and no other: *his* person, *his* teaching, *his* work, *his* destiny, all interpreted in the light of the holy scriptures. And it is most difficult to assume that this peculiar process of development first began after Easter. For my own part, I believe that the early Christian proclamation of Jesus as Messiah had deep factual roots in Jesus' own proclamation and in his own view of himself.

We have now reviewed the three major titles used in the early Christian interpretation of Christ. In every case I find it hard to discover an original core clearly different in kind from the motif we see in the mature Christology. What we do see here is a lively and changing process of development, but a development which is to a high degree *interpretive* in nature. We do not get the impression that early Christianity produced bold innovations and projected these backward in time. It rather seems that the early church interpreted creatively something given in the tradition concerning the Lord Jesus.

A few words should perhaps be added about the genesis of the Son of Man designation. This question, as is well known, is extremely complicated and controversial. The opinions of modern scholars are so diverse that one does not dare to hope for a consensus until some new manuscript has been discovered. I find it especially worth considering that early Christianity had so much difficulty in dealing with the Son of Man designation. In Greek-speaking areas it could hardly be used at all. It evidently was felt to be as clumsy and hard to understand as it was misleading. Nevertheless we find this awkward term in the sayings of Jesus in the Gospels—and nearly exclusively there. This can scarcely be explained otherwise than that the early Christians felt obligated to preserve a peculiarity in Jesus' own manner of speaking. The fact that this term in the course of time appeared ever more frequently in sayings of Jesus among the evangelists also indicates that it was considered to be *typical* for the speech of the Master. Here we have another token of conservatism and continuity in the Jesus tradition: even awkward expressions were preserved (though of course this was not always possible). We recognize again a parallel with rabbinic tradition. At the same time we can see from the content of the Son of Man texts that an interpretive development has taken place.

The question regarding continuity in the early Christian view of Jesus has a number of aspects, and one of them has, in my opinion, not received enough attention in the debate of the last generation about the history of the gospel tradition, or in the debate concerning the christological development in early Christianity. I am thinking of the *ethical* dimension in the early church's interpretation of Jesus. Much has been written during the last generation about the relationship between Jesus and the Old Testament prophecies, but remarkably little about the relationship between Jesus and the *Law*, the basic demands of Torah. I have sought to clarify this question in a series of studies during the past decade. I have been struck by the fact that an impressive number of the sayings of Jesus in the Gospels seem to have some relation to the summarizing commandment in the Torah: "Hear, O Israel: The Lord our God is one Lord; and you shall love the Lord your God with all your heart, and with all your soul, and with all your might" (Deut 6:4–5). It does seem obvious that Israel's creedal text (the Shema)—in which the command to love God is included—played a fundamental role for Jesus. And in the early Christian teaching about Jesus as the fulfiller of Torah this element has been well preserved. In this ethical dimension too there is an obvious unity, constancy, and continuity in the Jesus tradition. Unfortunately we cannot here examine this complicated problem more closely.[23]

XI. PERSONAL CONTINUITY IN EARLY CHRISTIANITY

For the pioneer form critics, Dibelius and Bultmann, it was a fundamental idea—taken over from contemporary folklore—that

---

[23] [See now my books *The Shema in the New Testament: Deut 6:4–5 in Significant Passages* (Lund: Novapress, 1996) and *The Ethos of the Bible* (Philadelphia: Fortress, 1981; London: Darton, Longman and Todd, 1982). For some reflections on the inclusive character of the New Testament Christology, see my article "The Christology of Matthew," in *Who Do You Say That I Am? Essays on Christology* (ed. M. A. Powell and D. R. Bauer; Louisville: Westminster John Knox, 1999), 14–32.]

the synoptic tradition had anonymous origins in the early Christian congregations, that it arose among people whose names are unknown. Dibelius compares the emergence and the history of this tradition to a biological process and quotes the phrase "a biology of the legend" *(eine Biologie der Sage)*. Bultmann agrees. Numerous scholars have opposed this point. Vincent Taylor remarks wryly in his book *The Formation of the Gospel Tradition:* "If the Form-Critics are right, the disciples must have been translated to heaven immediately after the Resurrection."[24] I would like to make some observations here about authorities and continuity of persons in early Christianity.

It is obvious that certain well-known sociopsychological mechanisms also functioned in early Christianity. We can establish, for example, that the early Christian congregations are nowhere described in our sources as gray masses of unnamed equals. Everywhere we see that certain persons have greater authority than others. And clearly one of the factors which gave a person authority in the early church was what he knew about Jesus.

In the New Testament Jesus is the authority with a capital *A;* he has no equal. But after his departure we find that Jesus' closest disciples are also granted a position of honor, and specifically because they have been with Jesus (cf. Acts 1:21–22). And it is of exceptional importance in this context that their relationship to Jesus is not depicted as a vague contact but as a direct disciple relationship. Jesus' closest adherents have not only seen and heard Jesus; they have received teaching from him directly. Thus we see that the first link in the chain of tradition—the one between Jesus and his first disciples—is described as a relationship characterized by instruction given and received.

That Jesus devoted himself to *teaching* is an original and everywhere confirmed datum of the gospel tradition in its entirety. If we survey the Gospels, and for the sake of simplicity disregard the question of the different layers in the material, we see this in many ways. Jesus' followers address him as rabbi *(rabbi),* master *(didaskalos, epistatēs),* or Lord *(Kyrios).* Those closest to him are called disciples *(mathētai).* He teaches both privately and publicly, both outdoors (at

---

[24]London: MacMillan & Co., 1933, 41.

the seashore, on a mountain, and so on) and indoors (in synagogues or private houses). He walks from town to town and teaches. The disciples "are with him" *(einai meta, einai syn)* constantly, on weekdays and Sabbaths. When Jesus makes his journeys, his disciples "follow" *(akolouthein)* him. They serve him in various ways. Admittedly their relationship to the Master is not specified with a verb meaning "to serve," but we see from circumstantial reports that they do assist Jesus in different ways and carry out errands on his behalf. It appears that the group closest to Jesus lives together in a certain house in Capernaum and even stays together when on their journeys. According to John (12:6; 13:29) they also share a common purse. When Mark records (in 3:14) the choosing of the Twelve, he tells us that Jesus "appointed twelve that they might be with him" *(hina ōsin met' autou)* and that he might send them out. From this formulation it appears that the evangelist intends to say that the Twelve constituted an inner group which Jesus, during his earthly ministry, had delimited and made his own spiritual family, his "house." We even find a tradition in which Jesus designates his disciples as his true family (Mark 3:31–35 and the parallels).

As is well known, there is a lively discussion today whether the collegium of the Twelve actually existed in Jesus' time, or whether Mark simply retrojects this early Christian group back into the life of Jesus. I find it very hard to believe that the collegium of the Twelve is secondary in the gospel tradition. One reason for this is the very role which these men play in the Gospels, for we quite clearly do not encounter here the mature, authoritative pillar figures who were looked up to in the early church. Here we meet twelve insignificant, immature disciples, lacking understanding and wisdom. If Mark had projected the Twelve backward to the time of Jesus, he must have been such a clever writer of history that he could at the same time bring these venerable spiritual leaders back to a strikingly youthful and immature stage. The basic hypothesis must thus be supported by a series of fabricated complementary hypotheses. The simplest solution, and therefore the one historically most probable, is that the Twelve actually were with Jesus during his earthly ministry.

If so, Jesus did not simply have a number of disciples. He had selected a group of twelve of them, given them a special position, and thereby a special authorization. This would provide a natural explanation of the great authority the Twelve exercised after Easter. I believe that such was the case. But I shall not proceed to argue on the basis of this judgment. Neither shall I get involved in the troublesome question regarding the early Christian *apostolate* and its connection with Jesus' authorization of the Twelve.[25] I content myself with pointing to the important continuity which had its basis in the fact that Jesus had *disciples,* who subsequently were able to function as experts who knew what the Master had said and done.

The man who wrote the Gospel of Luke and the book of Acts (I call him Luke) asserts in his famous prologue that the Jesus traditions which he has put together in his work go back to those "who from the beginning were eyewitnesses and ministers of the word." He thus characterizes the Jesus material as tradition (the verb used is *paradidonai*), and he indicates those who first bore the tradition. When he refers to those "who from the beginning were eyewitnesses and ministers of the word" *(autoptai kai hypēretai tou logou),* Luke is primarily thinking of the Twelve. They form the nucleus of those who were present "during all the time that the Lord Jesus went in and out among us" (Acts 1:21), and subsequently devoted themselves to "the ministry of the word" *(diakonia tou logou,* 6:4). They preach and teach and heal "in Jesus' name" (Acts 3:6; 4:10, 18; 5:28, 40, etc.). They appear as Jesus' "witnesses," witnesses above all to his resurrection. It is the "apostles' teaching" *(hē didachē tōn apostolōn,* Acts 2:42) which holds the believers together, and the early Christian community in Jerusalem—the mother congregation itself—grows around a nucleus composed of the Twelve and Jesus' mother and brothers.

It is quite clear that Luke provides us with a simplified and even tendentious picture; the beginnings of the early church were certainly a much more complicated process than Luke makes them out to be. But it is hard to deny that in certain basic respects he has the historical probabilities in his favor. Who would have taken up Jesus' fallen mantle after Easter if not his closest disciples? Who would have received greater respect as experts and witnesses than they? To whom would people go if they wanted to know what Jesus had said

---

[25] See my "Die Boten Gottes und die Apostel Christi," *Svensk Exegetisk Årsbok* 27 (1962): 89–131.

and done, and what really had happened when he was executed, *interpreted from within,* in the light of his own teaching?

At this point it is illuminating to take note of the simple mechanisms which functioned among the rabbis. If a person wanted to know what a given teacher, no longer living, actually taught, he would go to the teacher's disciples, to those who had heard him teach. Some people journeyed long in order to find out what a certain rabbi had taught on a given point. According to the rabbinical tradition, for example, the young Hillel traveled all the way from Babylon to Jerusalem in order to obtain information on a few issues.

It was not rank which made one a bearer of tradition. Sometimes it is asserted in the literature that only ordained rabbis could transmit the traditions. That is a purely arbitrary claim. Ordination did convey authority. But anyone who had heard and seen a teacher could (provided he was a responsible person with a tongue in his mouth) transmit what he knew. The rabbis often employed rather simple and insignificant assistants in this role. The prime requirement was that such persons had a dependable memory. In the old Mishnaic tractate *Eduyyot* we can see how old practice is ascertained by seeking out knowledgeable witnesses. The status of such persons is immaterial; their knowledge of the point at issue is all that matters. In one case a question was resolved on the basis of testimony provided by two weavers—simple artisans, in other words—who had heard what Shemaiah and Abtalion had said about a certain question (*Ed.* 1:3).

My contention is thus that we have every reason to proceed on the assumption that Jesus' closest disciples had an authoritative position in early Christianity as witnesses and bearers of the traditions of what Jesus had said and done. There is no reason to suppose that any believer in the early church could create traditions about Jesus and expect that his word would be accepted.

If we consider Paul, who was not himself one of Jesus' disciples during his earthly ministry and who therefore might seem an unlikely source of support for the points of view presented here, we find, contrary to expectation, significant information leading in the same direction. Even though he had to struggle energetically to assert his own freedom and sovereignty as an apostle, he nevertheless discloses something of the authoritative status of the mother congregation and its men of repute *(hoi dokountes)*—men such as Peter, James and John—and of the group in Jerusalem to whom he refers as "those who were apostles before me" (*hoi pro emou apostoloi,* Gal 1:17).

In 1 Corinthians Paul describes himself as a bearer of tradition. He has delivered to the congregations Jesus traditions which he has received himself. He stands therefore in a chain of tradition. In 1 Cor 4:14–17 we find (as noted above) a most interesting statement. Paul here admonishes the congregation in Corinth to imitate him as he imitates Christ; and, in order to assist the congregation in this regard, he sends to them his beloved and faithful son Timothy to remind them of his "ways," that is, the doctrines and practices he inculcates in all of his congregations. Thus we have here an example of tradition proceeding from an apostle to a congregation via the apostle's disciple. As we know, the postapostolic literature provides us with more examples of such chains of personal continuity in the early church—even though the gospel was being spread in book form as well by that time.

It is also important to remember the personal continuity which the evangelists themselves represent. The Gospels are not collections of tradition hundreds of years old. The Gospel of Mark was written no more than forty years after Jesus was crucified, the other three no more than thirty years after Mark. Mark at least wrote while many eyewitnesses were still living, and he evidently was personally acquainted with leading members of the Jesus circle in Jerusalem, as well as with Paul. The author of the Lukan writings is also probably a man named in the New Testament—the Luke who was Paul's coworker. Those behind the Gospels of Matthew and John are more difficult to identify. But in these cases too we have reason to believe that they had been in personal contact with eyewitnesses.

These perspectives have not been given due weight in the gospel research of the form-critical era. It seems as though parallels from folklore—that is, material extending over centuries and widely different geographical areas—have tempted scholars unconsciously to stretch out the chronological and geographical dimensions of the formation of the early Christian tradition in an unreasonable manner. What is needed here is a more sober approach to history. In the New Testament period the church was not nearly as widespread or as large in numbers as we usually imagine.

XII. FROM JESUS TO THE GOSPELS

I have previously touched upon one of the most perplexing aspects of the documents preserved from early Christianity: the isolation of the Jesus tradition. In the New Testament we have on the one hand the three Synoptic Gospels with traditions from and about Jesus. In them we find direct quotations of words Jesus is said to have spoken during his earthly ministry, and direct reports of what he is said to have done while at work in Israel. The mystery of Jesus is not presented here in the framework of proclamation, teaching, or admonition. We find here that a number of independent words and narratives have been brought together to form an orderly account of a bygone period in the history of salvation. The fact that there is an *edifying intention* in the evangelists' presentation in no way belies this assertion.

On the other hand, we find in the New Testament a number of letters written by early Christian authorities to Christian congregations in the period of the early church. They bear the names of Paul, Peter, John, James, and Jude. These letters give us a reasonable idea of how men preached, taught, and admonished in the first Christian communities. In these letters we find practically no direct quotations of what Jesus had said or reports of what he had done during his ministry. The authors seem to presuppose such material, to allude to it, to build further upon its content, to instruct in the same spirit, and so on, but they virtually never quote.

This simple state of affairs makes it very difficult for me to accept the assertion of the form critics that the synoptic tradition arose and was preserved in the general preaching, teaching, and exhortation of the early Christian congregations. Questions concerning where the evangelists got this *isolated* Jesus tradition and how it was handed on in the early church before the Gospels were written have not received acceptable answers from the form critics.

I have already pointed out that in 1 Corinthians (chs. 11 and 15) Paul seems to provide us with a clue to the answer to these questions. It seems from what Paul says in these two chapters that regular acts of transmitting texts occurred in early Christianity; that is, when the need arose, one or more Jesus traditions were handed on to a recipient, either in writing or by impressing the text upon the memory. If in writing, it must have been in the form of private notes: "scrolls of secrets," as the rabbis could call them, or "memoranda," as the Greek teachers referred to them, but not proper books. I find it likely that Paul is referring to oral transmission in these passages.

Now we shall pose this question: Can we perceive in the *Gospels* any indication that textual transmission of this kind was already taking place while Jesus was active in Galilee and Jerusalem?

If one examines the words of Jesus in the Synoptic Gospels—sayings and parables—one is struck by their artistic form. The English scholar C. F. Burney wrote a captivating book on this topic many years ago *(The Poetry of Our Lord).*[26] More recent authors have supplemented Burney's observations, among others, Joachim Jeremias.[27]

The sayings of Jesus in the Synoptic Gospels do not have the character of everyday words or of casual repartee. Nor can they be arbitrarily selected portions of sermons or of doctrinal discourses. Rather they consist of brief, laconic, well-rounded texts, of pointed statements with a clear profile, rich in content and artistic in form. The artistic devices show through clearly even in the tradition's Greek form: picturesque content, strophic construction, *parallelismus membrorum,* verbatim repetitions, and so on. These features can be seen all the more clearly if one translates back into Aramaic. Then one sees in the sayings of Jesus such characteristics as rhythm, assonance, and alliteration as well. It is obvious that we are dealing here with carefully thought out and deliberately formulated statements.

We can also see in the Gospels that early Christianity had a summary designation for texts of this kind. In Greek they were called *parabolai* (pl.). The term is used not only in reference to narrative parables of various kinds (e.g., Matt 13), but also in reference to brief word pictures and sayings (e.g., the saying, "There is nothing outside a man which by going into him can defile him," Mark 7:15, 17; cf. 4:33 and Luke 4:23). It was typical of Jesus' way of teaching to do so with the aid of *parabolai* (cf. Mark 4:2a).

---

[26] *The Poetry of Our Lord: An Examination of the Formal Elements of Hebrew Poetry in the Discourses of Jesus Christ* (Oxford: Oxford University Press, 1925).

[27] See, e.g., *Neutestamentliche Theologie* (Gütersloh: Gütersloher Verlagshaus, 1971), part I, 124–38; ET *New Testament Theology* (trans. J. Bowden; New York: Scribner's Sons, 1971), 14–29.

Behind the Greek *parabolē* (sing.) are the Hebrew *māshāl* (pl. *meshālim* or *meshālot*) and the Aramaic *matlā'*. These words were used for picturesque sayings, whether they were very short or somewhat longer, as distinct from more ordinary, everyday speech: a metaphor, a parable, an allegory, a fable, a maxim, a riddle, a folk song, or whatever. As we know, the proverbs in the book of Proverbs are called *meshālim,* the book's Hebrew name is *Mishle Shelomoh* (Solomon's meshalim). In the Old Testament we also find an old designation for the men who were known for their ability to transmit traditional words of wisdom and to formulate sayings of their own. They were called *moshelim,* that is, tellers of parables, makers of proverbs, men of pithy speech.

What we see here is how Jesus' teaching can be judged from a *purely formal* point of view. He did not teach in such a way that he can be classified as a teacher of the law (a halakist). One might classify him as a haggadist, inasmuch as the term *haggādāh* was sufficiently vague to be applicable to all nonjuridical teaching. But that classification is not very helpful; one can be more precise. According to the express testimony of the early Christian sources, Jesus taught with the aid of *meshālim,* in Greek *parabolai,* that is, parables and sayings. He was—if we may employ an ancient designation—a *moshel,* a parabolist, one who spoke in parables and pithy sayings.

This does not mean that he was purely and simply a popular wisdom teacher of the old type. From the content of his teaching we see that he at times could utilize traditional wisdom, but for the most part he spoke in his own original way about the reign of God, both of its external, obvious characteristics and of its inner secrets, its "mysteries." He had a message—the kerygma concerning the reign of God—and he presented it with the aid of parables and sayings (as well as deeds). We also note that this was done in a prophetic spirit, and with messianic authority. Jesus appears in the Synoptic Gospels as a personage who combines a variety of traits from the ancient heritage of Israel's various men of God. And he is not simply one teacher among many. He breaks through the usual categories. It is typical that he is described as "more than" Solomon, "more than" Jonah, David's "Lord," and so on. When I describe him as a *moshel* (a parabolist) I do so simply to characterize from a purely *formal* point of view the way in which he shaped his oral teaching.

If we analyze this type of saying, we note that the wording itself is of great importance. The intent here is not simply to instruct or to clarify in general terms, but to provide the listeners with certain words to ponder and discuss. The speaker in this context does not engage his hearers in conversation, nor does he lecture them, but rather presents them with a parable; he delivers a proverb to them. They receive it somewhat in the way one receives a curious object which one must examine in order to find out how it can be used. They are given a text upon which they can ruminate and which they can discuss with one another in an effort to find its meaning. What is most important here, of course, is not that people learn the text, but that they understand its meaning—but the meaning is dependent on the wording.

If one looks at the *form* which these sayings take, one notes that they are brief, pointed, and pregnant. The sayings have been formulated so that they can be easily remembered. As we know, the Gospels tell us that Jesus "spoke in meshalim (parables)," "taught in meshalim," or "set forth a mashal" for his listeners. Such statements can scarcely mean that Jesus presented the text in question only once, expecting that those who heard it would remember it and be able to understand it. In the light of the ancient Jewish methods of teaching, it seems clear to me that Jesus presented such a saying two or more times in an effort to impress it upon the minds ("hearts") of his hearers. Among the rabbis we can see how evident it was that a teacher would repeat the texts until his pupils knew them by heart; four repetitions seems to have been common.

The evangelists maintain that Jesus regularly presented meshalim in his public teaching and when necessary *interpreted* these for his disciples. This applies both to meshalim of the type we call parables (e.g., Mark 4; Matt 13; Luke 8) and to those we call logia (e.g., Mark 7; Matt 15). The evangelists thus describe not only occasions on which Jesus presents such texts, but also situations in which he comments upon them; note for example such terms as *epilyein* (explain, interpret) in Mark 4:34; *diasaphein* (explain, expound) in Matt 13:36; *phrazein* (interpret) in Matt 15:15. One cannot exclude the possibility that the scenes described in the parable chapter and in the chapter dealing with clean and unclean eating were drawn up for the first time at a later stage. But there are scarcely tenable grounds for the suspicion that the teaching pattern as such lacks historical foundation.[28] Here we cannot be dealing with a simple backdating of teaching scenes from the time of the early church. And there is no reason to believe that texts of this kind were of interest only after Easter. If Jesus created meshalim during his public ministry, it is reasonable to assume that his disciples preserved these texts right from the beginning. They must have fixed them in their memories, pondered them, and discussed them. Otherwise they were not his disciples. Why would the disciples not have been interested in these texts *prior to Easter?*

In an essay by Heinz Schürmann which I mentioned earlier ("Die vorösterlichen Anfänge der Logientradition"), the author has emphasized that even from a purely form-critical point of view one must reckon with the fact that Jesus' followers began to preserve a tradition of sayings already before Easter. He refers among other things to the fact that according to the Gospels Jesus, during his ministry in Galilee, sent out his disciples to preach and to heal. This sending has such a strong anchoring in the tradition that, all things being considered, it cannot be dismissed as a simple backdating of the early Christian missionary activity after Easter (Mark 6:7–13 and parallels; Luke 10:1–16). Schürmann points out that Jesus must have given these immature and unlearned disciples certain instructions about what they were to preach before he sent them out. Here then is a situation in which we must assume that Jesus imprinted his teaching in the minds of his disciples.

To this I would add that all teaching in meshalim must reasonably be of this kind. If Jesus taught in parables and logia, in all probability he taught his hearers these texts. My contention is that the very form of the sayings of Jesus indicates that they were never *integrated* parts of a broad, continuous presentation. And I maintain for that reason that nothing suggests that these words were of interest only after Easter. On the contrary, everything suggests that devoted disciples memorized them already at the time their master taught them during his ministry in Galilee and Jerusalem.

Here then we have a point of departure. Jesus presented meshalim for his hearers, and the disciples were the first to memorize

---

[28] See David Daube, *The New Testament and Rabbinic Judaism* (London: Athlone, 1956; repr. Peabody, Mass.: Hendrickson, n.d.), 141–50.

them, to ponder them, and to discuss together what they meant. In the beginning was Jesus' kerygma concerning the reign of God. The oldest components in the gospel tradition are certainly in principle the logia and the parables which served to make this kerygma concrete and understandable.

Since the disciples had begun to preserve Jesus' teachings in this way, it was quite natural that *narrative texts about Jesus* also appeared in order to supplement the meshalim. An intermediary form between the sayings tradition and the narrative tradition consists of those elements in the tradition which Dibelius calls paradigms and Bultmann apothegms. These are sayings of Jesus which are provided with a brief narrative introduction. The sayings themselves are certainly the most important here, but disciples have in many cases put them in context, briefly indicating the situation in which they were uttered, in order to make them comprehensible. It is easy to imagine how such expanded sayings traditions were added to the memorized material. And from the apothegms it is not far to those elements in the tradition which sum up a conversation.

As far as the narrative material proper is concerned, it is also easy to imagine how certain elements soon came into the picture. I am thinking of reports of certain things which Jesus had done and which were understood to be symbolic actions. Here the mashal lay in the deed itself, but if one wanted to prompt another who had not seen what was done to think about its meaning and discuss it, then it was obviously necessary to formulate a report about the deed.

It is not possible to treat all narrative traditions in one and the same way. The detailed, vivid accounts which Dibelius refers to as tales *(Novellen)* provide particular problems in this context. Nonetheless, I think that one can easily imagine how the narrative traditions quite naturally came to supplement the sayings traditions. Jesus had not presented himself in word alone. He had also done a number of characteristic deeds. He was known as one who could miraculously heal the sick and expel demons. It would have been unnatural to preserve only the sayings of such a man.

With regard to the Passion story, the groundwork of the narrative was certainly laid soon after Easter, for early Christianity had here received its most puzzling mashal: Why was it necessary for Jesus to "suffer these things and enter into his glory" (cf. Luke 24:26)?

The clarity to which the early church came with regard to the meaning of the suffering, death, and resurrection of Jesus was accompanied by a clarity as to his identity and peculiar status as Messiah. Now a full picture of Jesus had emerged and it was possible to interpret the individual traditions in the light of a strong, unified conviction about who Jesus actually was, and to organize the tradition material on the basis of all-encompassing principles. It would be hard to prove that this insight was first gained in the Hellenistic branch of Christianity. I also find it difficult to prove that the church's understanding of the mystery of Jesus after Easter was a fundamentally *different* picture from the provisional one which Jesus had sought to give to his disciples during his days on earth (even though many misunderstandings obviously remained at the time of the crucifixion). In principle it seems to be only a clearer and more complete picture. The same holds true of the relationship between Jesus' kerygma of the reign of God and the church's post-Easter kerygma. The church's kerygma about Christ was by all the evidence little other than a more concrete, precise, and fully developed version of Jesus' message about the reign of God. The enigmatic could now—at least in part—be proclaimed clearly.

When we speak of the *connection* between the individual elements in the tradition, it is important that we do not limit our perspective to the form-critical thesis that the separate elements arose completely independently of one another and stood from the beginning entirely on their own without any inner, organic relationship. That does not seem to have been the case. A number of scholars, including C. H. Dodd, H. Riesenfeld, and H. Simonsen, have demonstrated that many of the tradition elements in the Gospels quite simply presuppose others or point ahead to others. Furthermore, one sees time after time that the early Christian traditionist knew more about Jesus than he could have derived directly from the wording of the tradition elements. Relevant here are the many observations which point to the fact that early Christianity already had, in its earliest phase of development, a general picture of Jesus and a rough outline of his life's course, with emphasis on his death and resurrection. New audiences had to be provided with this orientation.

These observations deserve our careful attention if we wish to have a balanced understanding of the origin and history of the synoptic tradition. It will not do to *limit* one's perspective to the idea that the individual elements in the tradition are prior to the redactional patterns used in gathering the materials. The history of the origins of the synoptic tradition is not only the history of how the various parts arose and were assembled, but also the history of *the interaction between the whole and the parts,* between the total view and the concrete formation of the material, which certainly took place during the entire tradition formation process.

A further problem of relevance here concerns the transition from oral tradition to writings. This was certainly a drawn-out and involved process. As I have already suggested, private notes were probably made rather early. As time went on, blocks of tradition, large and small, have been put together, and eventually the time was ripe for the first gospel in our sense of the word. This whole area is full of difficult questions. For example, what happens when oral tradition of just this kind is put into writing? How in such cases does tradition subsequently influence what is written? And how does what is written influence tradition? The influence here is obviously reciprocal. I cannot, however, pursue this further at this time.

I do not believe that there is any *simple* answer to the question concerning the origins of the gospel tradition. There is certainly a complicated development behind our Synoptic Gospels—to say nothing about the Gospel of John, which, as far as I can see, has its own history. But I believe that there is historical justification, based on sound historical judgments, for concluding that there is an unbroken path which leads from Jesus' teaching in meshalim to the early church's methodical handing on of Jesus texts, a transmission carried on for *its own sake.* In other words, this was done not only in order that the recipients might come to faith or be strengthened in their love, but also for the specific reason that they should *have* these indispensable texts. I am referring to those activities in early Christianity by which Jesus texts were transmitted, either orally or in writing. Paul discloses in 1 Corinthians 11 and 15 that such took place. History does not follow only theological lines. As a historian, one must pay attention to trivial and practical circumstances as well. The early Christian congregations did not live only on preaching and theology. They had practical things to see about too, such as procuring sacred scriptures. They had also, I contend, quite practically to secure Jesus tradition for themselves, and this in spite of the fact that faith comes neither by copying texts nor by memorizing them.

XIII. "THE WHOLE TRUTH"

In what has been written to this point I have attempted in a brief, outline manner to indicate why I believe that the Gospels essentially provide us with a historically reliable picture of Jesus of Nazareth. This applies primarily to the Synoptic Gospels. Among other reasons, the four following arguments speak in favor of the view that the continuity and reliability of the early Christian tradition have been preserved without interruption:

(1) The early Christian congregations were not shapeless communities in which spiritual goods were created anonymously. All the sources from early Christianity indicate that already in its first stages certain leaders and teachers occupied positions of authority in the congregations and that these men were in contact with one another. The Twelve, with Peter at their head, had a central authority which even Paul had to take into account. We can see chains of tradition delineated in the material: Peter was Jesus' disciple, Paul knew Peter (Gal 1:18; 2:1–14), Timothy was Paul's disciple (1 Cor 4:16–17), and so on.

(2) In the Synoptic Gospels, no later "high Christology" has been able to efface the characteristic picture of an earthly Jesus. Typical features of his appearance in Israel have been preserved: he appears with power *(exousia)* as a mysterious but authoritative representative of the coming reign of God; he proclaims that reign (in the form of meshalim); he expounds God's demands on those who are to enter the reign; he heals sick people, expels demons, and sets this activity in relation to the reign of God; he is generous to the religious and social outcasts in Israel to the point of giving offence, which is not the least of the reasons why he comes in conflict with the leaders of his people; he dies for his cause and that of the reign of God, and so on. This is no simple backdating of the faith in Christ manifested in the church after Easter.

(3) One feature which sharply distinguishes the formation of the early Christian tradition from the formation of popular traditions in general is that the former takes place in continuous contact with authoritative sacred scriptures. Jesus himself taught in association with the holy scriptures, and the synoptic material clearly had this same association the whole time until it was finally written down. This association had an enriching but obviously also a stabilizing effect on the tradition.[29]

(4) Even with regard to the wording of the Jesus tradition—and here primarily that of the sayings tradition—the Gospels reflect the fact that the material has been preserved with respect and care.

The sources give us no reason to believe that just anyone in the early Christian period could say that Jesus had said anything whatever. I maintain that Jesus' closest disciples—Peter, James, John, and the group known as the Twelve—must be suspected of having had much to do with the oldest stages of the synoptic tradition. They preserved Jesus' meshalim—logia, parables—and began to tell of his activities even while he was conducting his own ministry before Easter.

It is difficult to answer the question to what extent the synoptic material was assembled in various collections by the Twelve during their activity in Jerusalem in the first phase of the mother congregation there. Luke's presentation in his gospel (1:1–4) and in the book of Acts has an a priori probability at its center: who would have continued the Master's work if not the members of his innermost circle of disciples? But Luke obviously provides a highly simplified, tendentious, and stylized picture of a complicated historical process. There certainly were persons "working with the word" in congregations other than the one in Jerusalem; they too preserved words of Jesus and narratives about him, discussed and interpreted them, and all of this in connection with an intensive study of the holy scriptures (cf. Acts 17:11). None of the evangelists worked with traditions taken only from one source.

It thus seems historically very probable that the Jesus traditions in the Gospels have been preserved for us by persons both reliable and well informed. But even the one who has come to this point of

---

[29] Cf. Ellis, "New Directions in Form Criticism" (n. 13), 299–315.

view sees directly in our gospels that the Jesus traditions must have undergone certain changes on the way from Jesus to the different evangelists. If one places the three synoptic versions side by side— that is, by looking in a synopsis—one can see immediately how they differ from one another. It is thus uncontestable that changes took place in this material in the process of its transmission (as well as in its final redaction). The only question is how extensive these changes can have been. We shall now in conclusion touch briefly upon this issue.

A number of factors brought about the changes in this material, but it is not necessary to list them all now. One important factor to keep in mind is the *transfer of the material* from Aramaic and Hebrew *to Greek*. Admittedly this occurred in a multilingual milieu, where the traditions were found side by side in the original language and in Greek and where so many people knew both languages that the translations could for a long time be checked and corrected. Nonetheless it is well known that no translation can be completely identical with the original and that two or more translations will never be word for word the same. The prologue to the book of Sirach indicates that these observations are not new.

Particularly significant changes can hardly have taken place at the translation into Greek, however. Greater significance must be attached to the changes which occurred during the ongoing *interpretation* of the traditions, in the efforts to understand Jesus' words and deeds more fully and comprehensively and to discover their importance for the problems and questions which confronted the congregations in their day. There are clear signs of this activity in the Gospels, indications of what we can call early Christianity's "work with the word of the Lord."

In each of the Gospels we see reflected the early church's consciousness of the fact that Jesus' closest followers did not understand him particularly well during his earthly ministry—not only his predictions of his imminent suffering and violent death were difficult to comprehend—and that many aspects of his secret did not dawn upon them until after Easter. A couple of quotations from the Gospel of John put this in a nutshell. In John 12:12–16 the evangelist reports on Jesus' entry into Jerusalem. He makes this comment: "His disciples did not understand this at first, but when

Jesus was glorified, then they remembered that this had been written of him and had been done to him." In 2:19–22 Jesus, in the course of his teaching in Jerusalem, pronounces the logion concerning the destruction of the temple and its rebuilding in three days. Afterward John comments: "When therefore he was raised from the dead, his disciples remembered that he had said this; and they believed the scripture and the word which Jesus had spoken." Here we see how conscious the evangelist is of the fact that certain of Jesus' words and deeds were not clear to the disciples until after the resurrection. We note further that the interpretation of Jesus' words and of what happened to him is connected with the interpretation of the sacred scriptures.

John (I call the man behind the Fourth Gospel by this name without going into the question who he really was) gives us his own explanation of the fact that the church understands Jesus more fully after Easter. In his farewell address, the Johannine Jesus says: "But the Counselor, the Holy Spirit, whom the Father will send in my name, he will teach you all things, and bring to your remembrance all that I have said to you" (14:26). And later on, in this same farewell speech, Jesus says: "When the Spirit of truth comes, he will guide you into the whole truth . . . He will glorify me, for he will take what is mine and declare it to you" (16:13–14).

These passages (and several similar ones) in the Gospel of John provide us with insights into the way in which the post-Easter situation is seen from within the Johannine circle. We see here the deliberateness with which they work with the Jesus tradition, striving better to understand both it and the sacred scriptures. They feel that the Lord himself has authorized them to do this, the Lord who has been glorified and who has sent his Spirit to guide the church into "the whole truth." In this situation, and with this conviction, they feel free to develop and embellish the content of the Jesus tradition. To them it is the Spirit who leads the church into "the whole truth"! In the Johannine congregations the margin for the free rendering of the significance of Jesus' words appears to have been remarkably large. The Johannine Jesus seems to be speaking through the mouth of his early Christian interpreters. To put it in rabbinical terms, one could say that the early Christian interpreters *(meturgemānin)* here stand between us and the laconic, earthly Jesus.

Nevertheless, there is in the Gospel of John an express desire to stand firmly on historical ground. When the evangelist at the original conclusion of the Gospel (20:30–31)—chapter 21 is, as we know, an appendix—writes about the purpose of the book, he says: "Now Jesus did many other signs in the presence of the disciples, which are not written in this book; but these are written that you may believe that Jesus is the Christ, the Son of God, and that believing, you may have life in his name." The evangelist writes with a clear tendentiousness: the faith of his readers is to be preserved and strengthened. But he intends to present that which Jesus did "in the presence of the disciples." The degree to which the evangelist's presentation of the tradition material has been governed by his edifying tendentiousness can be seen rather clearly in the individual pericopes in the Fourth Gospel.

It is well known that the differences between the Gospel of John and the Synoptic Gospels are significant. John seems in certain essential respects to have built upon a different branch of the tradition than the synopticists, and to have treated the tradition material much more freely than the writers behind the Synoptics felt free to do. At the same time, however, the clues given in John's Gospel seem to be of help as we seek to clarify the history of the synoptic tradition as well.

It is entirely clear that the elements of the synoptic tradition have been open to changes of *one* kind: those made in an effort to clarify the *meaning* of the transmitted texts, to bring out "the whole truth" for the Christian congregations. I usually label changes of this kind *interpretive adaptations.* Even where the sayings of Jesus are concerned, it seems that liberty to make minor alterations in the wording in an effort to bring out the meaning was permitted (note, e.g., the various predictions of suffering). Nothing has hindered the creation in this way of several variants of one and the same Jesus saying, which have been preserved since they were all thought worth keeping. We often see, however, that the various interpretations of one and the same Jesus saying have been brought out by the evangelist primarily by placing the saying in a certain context or by reformulating the notices in the framework and the narrative material in the Gospels. These parts of the material have been reshaped with significantly greater liberty than the wording of the sayings of Jesus themselves.

Is not the observation that the Jesus traditions have undergone alterations all the evidence one needs to refute the thesis that early Christianity has handed down the gospel material as memorized texts? Many think so, but I have never understood this objection. We can see even in the rabbinical tradition that the material was altered in the course of time. Even in the collections of legal regulations, which are usually passed on with an extreme regard for the precise wording, changes do occur. Additions and subtractions were made.[30] Careful transmission thus does not prevent teachers with authority from making editorial alterations in texts and collections of texts. And if we proceed from halakic collections of traditions to other types of texts—those with midrashic and haggadic materials (logia, parables, etc.)—we note that the wording can vary even more. Careful oral transmission—with texts learned by heart—thus does not exclude alterations in texts. What often happens here is an interaction between transmission and editorial alteration.

If one compares the different versions of one and the same tradition in the Synoptic Gospels, one notes that the variations are seldom so general as to give us reason to speak of a fluid tradition which gradually became fixed. The alterations are not of the nature they would have been had originally elastic material been formulated in different ways. The tradition elements seem to have possessed a remarkably fixed wording. Variations generally take the form of additions, omissions, transpositions, or alterations of single details in a wording which otherwise is left unchanged. (I here ignore instances in which the evangelist has restructured an entire text.) The English scholar T. W. Manson once wrote with his usual pertinence that the early church "remembered better than it understood." The preservation of the wording of the texts and the interpretation of their meaning seem not always to have kept the same pace. This is an observation which is easily explained if the material transmitted is in the form of fixed texts handed down either in written or oral—memorized—form, or in both forms.

The apostles and teachers of early Christianity have thus stood in the situation where they were to preach about a Lord alive in the

---

[30] See *Memory and Manuscript* (n. 5), 77–78, 97–98, 111, 136–39, 146–48, 180–81, 334–35.

present but also proclaim that a significant part of this Lord's saving activity had been carried out in the past (albeit rather recently), and that here on earth, in Israel. It was important both to present a true picture of this work and to give it an adequate interpretation for the present. Early Christianity had reason both to preserve the Jesus tradition faithfully and to interpret it with insight. The incentive for both was great.

How large a margin for reformulation and renewal of the text traditions did the persons behind the synoptic tradition have? How much freedom did they feel to transform, and to introduce explanatory elements into the Jesus tradition? I believe that this margin was in general rather limited, but there are tradition elements which indicate that now and then remarkably large liberties could be taken.

I have investigated, for example, the long version of the narrative of how Jesus is tested by the devil after being baptized, in Matt 4:1–11 and Luke 4:1–13.[31] The account appears to be a tradition from Jesus' earthly activity, even though he is not yet surrounded by disciples. And it seems to contain certain undeniably historical elements: that Jesus was baptized by John the Baptist may be considered a reliable historical fact; nor is it improbable that Jesus went out into the wilderness for a time after the baptism, and that this was a time of testing for him. But otherwise the long version of "the temptation story" must be throughout a creation of certain early Christian scribes. It is a prologue to Jesus' public ministry in Israel. For the readers of the Gospel it serves to clarify the mystery that Jesus did not intend to "seek his own good" but to accomplish the will of God in word and deed, as it is revealed in the Torah. To be more precise, the account is designed to show that Jesus has heard and understood and is prepared to observe (or "to do") the summary commandment in Torah (Deut 6:4–5): "Hear, o Israel: the Lord our God is one Lord; and you shall love the Lord your God with all your heart [the first temptation], and with all your soul [the second temptation], and with all your might [the third temptation]." In a case like this the early Christian interpretation of the Jesus tradition has been

---

[31] *The Testing of God's Son (Matt 4:1–11 & Par.): An Analysis of an Early Christian Midrash* (ConBNT 2:1; Lund: Gleerup, 1966, now Stockholm: Almqvist & Wiksell International).

remarkably free and creative in character. The earliest tradition did provide points of contact—there *was something to interpret*—but in this instance it was interpreted with artistic freedom.

Now it is possible to explain this kind of element in the gospel tradition. We can see in the Jewish targum tradition that those who translated the old Hebrew texts into the Aramaic of the people in the worship services could when necessary introduce interpretations into their translations. They clearly saw—or heard—what the Hebrew did and did not say. Nonetheless they could inject interpretive elements into the text, even brief stories, in an effort to clarify its meaning. In a book about the baptism of Jesus, Fritzleo Lentzen-Deis has shed some very helpful light on this matter.[32] It seems that the early Christian traditionists took this same type of liberty on occasion, as, for example, when they reported on the baptism and testing of Jesus. The Matthean and Lukan versions of the temptation narrative reveal this. I am still not quite clear about the number of texts in the Synoptic Gospels that belong in this advanced category. Presumably there are not many. The temptation story is in many respects unique. But the fact that this account is found in the Synoptic Gospels tells us that early Christians occasionally permitted themselves to take great liberties—or, shall we say, use great creativity—in their efforts not only to hand down the texts of what Jesus had said and done, but also to interpret their mysteries for the listening congregation.

Thus there can be no doubt but that the Jesus traditions in the Synoptic Gospels have undergone revisions within the early church on their way from Jesus to the evangelists. Nor can there be any doubt but that the evangelists themselves have revised their material; all who have looked into this with open eyes know this. The most interesting and significant alterations in the tradition elements and additions to the collections result, as I understand it, from the desire of the early church to *understand* the transmitted material more deeply and comprehensively and to present it as clearly as possible to those who heard the gospel. That the congregations' current needs and problems influenced this process of interpretation is in the very

---

[32] *Die Taufe Jesu nach den Synoptikern: Literarkritische und gattungs-geschichtliche Untersuchungen* (FTS 4; Frankfurt a.M.: Knecht, 1970).

nature of the case; among the merits of the form critics is the fact that they have increased our awareness of this.

Insights and convictions which gradually came to the fore in the early years of Christian history have thus colored the old material derived from Jesus' ministry. To assert this does not mean, however, that one has adopted the attitude of the skeptical form critics. It is one thing to take these changes in the transmitted material in all seriousness, and quite another thing to presume that the early church freely constructed the Jesus traditions, placed the words of early Christian prophets and teachers in Jesus' mouth, and so on. One can say—with a degree of simplification—that the form critics (at least in the case of Bultmann and his disciples) have regarded the synoptic tradition as a post-Easter creation of the early church. My position is that one must proceed on the belief that the synoptic material in principle comes from the earthly Jesus and the disciples who followed him during his ministry, but that one must also do full justice to the fact that this memory material has been marked by the insights and interpretations gradually arrived at by the early Christian teachers.

I have been able, within the framework of these lectures, to do no more than *sketch* my position regarding the question of the historical credibility of the Gospels. It has not been possible to discuss the details of statements made about Jesus in the Gospels. Nevertheless, I hope that I have been able to point to reasons for the conclusion that in the Synoptic Gospels we hear not merely a whisper of the voice of Jesus, but are confronted with faithfully preserved words from his mouth and reports which *in the end* go back to those who were with him during his ministry in Galilee and Jerusalem. It is true that the accounts of Jesus' life and, to a certain degree, even a number of his sayings have been reworked by the early church, but the primary goal in all of this has been to understand them better.

In order to prevent misunderstanding, I should perhaps add an observation of a theological nature. If our desire is to understand *the original nature of Christian faith,* it is of decisive importance for us to study carefully the development of the Jesus tradition after Easter, that is, between the time of Jesus' earthly ministry and the time when the evangelists wrote the Gospels. We must also be clear about the message—in its entirety and in its parts—of the different evangelists themselves as it is seen in its final, fixed form. In other words, we must not look upon the tradition's development and alteration as a trivial process, without importance, nor as a corruption of something that was clearest when Jesus walked about in Galilee. The evangelists tell us repeatedly that the earthly Jesus was a riddle to his people and, to a large extent, even to his disciples. Their understanding of him and his message was, before Easter, imperfect and provisional. It was not until after Easter that the disciples thought they had achieved a clear and fully adequate understanding of the mystery of Jesus. It was only then that they recognized the complete meaning of the confession "You are the Christ, the Son of the living God." It was only then that they could see with full clarity Jesus' own place in the kerygma of the reign of God: his death and resurrection took a central place in the mysteries of the reign.

This increased clarity influenced the Jesus tradition. For this reason, one of the major tasks of the New Testament theologian is the analysis of the Jesus tradition's alterations and development, the study of the process which led Jesus' disciples to "the whole truth," to use John's words. Today, presumably, we can see more clearly than at the beginning of Christian history how *diversified* this "whole truth" was within the different congregations in the early church. But we can also see unity in the midst of this diversity. If the tradition did in fact develop roughly as I have sought to sketch above, then we can maintain that the different voices in the early church's mixed choir wanted to sing a common song: the song about the incomparable One, who has been elevated by God to the heavenly realm, but only after a mysterious ministry on earth.

II

꧁

The Path of the Gospel Tradition

I. THE ISOLATED JESUS TRADITION

New Testament studies is a discipline which has to move forward gropingly. We are forced to work with many learned conjectures, to establish the identity of fictive sources, and to reconstruct hypothetically the course of events behind these sources. We have to form a total picture of Jesus which is largely hypothetical. In a sense which is not exactly comfortable our discipline is a study of "things not seen."

Certainly, we do have *something* that is completely visible: the New Testament scriptures: four depictions of the earthly work of Jesus; a theological chronicle about the spread of the gospel from Jerusalem to Rome, the world metropolis; twenty-one genuine or fictional letters to early Christian churches or persons; and an apocalypse.

It is apparent—even striking—that, viewed from a fundamental perspective, these twenty-seven documents fall into two very distinct groups. When we look around for direct quotations from Jesus and concrete stories about his actions and fate during his years on earth, we find them in only one of these text groups: the Gospels. One can even push the matter to the extreme and say that the four gospels aim to transmit to us only words of Jesus and stories about Jesus, nothing else. To be sure, what they tell us about Jesus is set in the light of Easter and Pentecost and is often stated in relation to post-Easter circumstances and questions; they aim nonetheless to offer a picture of what Jesus did and taught during his earthly ministry (cf. Acts 1:1 and Luke 1:1–4). It is also true that the material of

John's Gospel represents a vigorous development, one that borders on free apostolic preaching, but even this gospel claims that it is portraying that which Jesus did before the eyes of his disciples on earth before his ascension to heaven (20:30; cf. 21:24–25). Here I shall refer to this gospel only incidentally; its peculiar character requires separate treatment.[1]

It is the purpose of the Gospels to furnish only concrete Jesus texts. When on the other hand we turn to the remaining twenty-three documents, we could say in an equally oversimplifying way that they essentially offer no concrete Jesus tradition at all. These documents were written in the spirit of Jesus and bear the stamp of his views and message. They contain allusions to his words and reminiscences of them, overarching pronouncements concerning his person, his life, and his work, above all concerning his death and resurrection, together with summaries and brief formulas. But none of these documents aims, in a foundational way, to give its readers a written account of what Jesus "did and taught" during his ministry on earth.

The exceptions are not hard to enumerate. In Acts 20:35 Paul reminds the elders of Ephesus of an (apocryphal) saying of Jesus. In 1 Cor 11:23–25 Paul aims to remind the Corinthian church of the words of Jesus concerning the elements of the Lord's Supper and to that end he repeats the pericope about Jesus' last meal with his disciples. And in 1 Cor 15:3–8 Paul once more repeats a summarizing text stating the fundamentals of the history of Jesus' death and resurrection. This text is a marginal case; nevertheless it is an instance of a firm text which restates concrete reminiscences of the work and fate of Jesus on earth.[2]

---

[1] Cf. J. D. G. Dunn's essay "Let John Be John: A Gospel for Its Time," in *The Gospel and the Gospels* (ed. P. Stuhlmacher; Grand Rapids: Eerdmans, 1991), 293–322. The German original bears the title *Das Evangelium und die Evangelien: Vorträge vom Tübinger Symposium 1982* (WUNT 28; Tübingen: Mohr [Siebeck], 1983).

[2] A borderline case: on the one hand the episodes referred to are not presented here in narrative form but only enumerated in chronological sequence, and on the other, the text does not seem to be complete; it lacks both introduction and conclusion. Cf. *Memory and Manuscript: Oral Tradition and Written Transmission in Rabbinic Judaism and Early Christianity*

The old distinction made in the church between *Euangelion* and *Apostolos* is terminologically vague and misleading—yet objectively fully justified. Only the evangelists seek to hand down proper gospel tradition to us. In the New Testament the concrete Jesus tradition, preserved in the form of self-contained small textual units, is present only in the Gospels, only as an isolated tradition.[3]

How does one explain this? Apostles, prophets, and teachers in early Christianity acted in their public ministry with authority and boldness and spoke freely about Jesus. They were neither forced anxiously to read from written texts nor restricted to commenting on them. In all the documents outside the Gospels we see how freely they could speak about Jesus. Where do we find the real Jesus tradition?

I can content myself by mentioning a couple of proposed solutions to the problem. One is that the Gospels quite simply are documents that have been composed at a late date, having been created freely and having no firm tradition behind their text. Another proposal is that the synoptic traditions were maintained only in an isolated part of primitive Christianity, in circles with which the other New Testament authors had no real contact. I consider both theses impossible. It seems to me almost inconceivable that the major part of early Christianity would not have been interested in knowing something concrete about Jesus' suffering, death, and resurrection, nor about his preceding activity, his words and teaching. All New Testament groups we know of gave their Lord in heaven the name Jesus, a quite ordinary *human* name,[4] and they also knew that he had lived a human life on earth.

We must look for the solution in another direction. The author of Acts intimates that he was familiar with the life and work of Jesus,

---

(ASNU 22; Lund: Gleerup, 1961), 299–300 [now in a new edition together with the booklet *Tradition and Transmission in Early Christianity* (Grand Rapids: Eerdmans, & Livonia: Dove, 1998), ibid.].

[3] In this essay the word "tradition" is used for that which is handed down, not for the act of transmission. The terms "gospel tradition" and "concrete Jesus tradition" are used synonymously of texts which contain sayings attributed to the earthly Jesus and narratives about him.

[4] Interesting observations about the history of the name "Jesus" are made by K. Kjær-Hansen in *Studier i navnet Jesus* (Aarhus: Menighedsfakultetet, 1982; English summary on pp. 369–81).

but he does not write in a way which lets us know that in reality he had a detailed knowledge of Jesus' words and deeds. The author of 1 John must have been quite familiar at the very least with the Johannine Jesus tradition—if he is not simply to be identified with the evangelist John himself—yet not even once does he expressly cite a word from Jesus (the quite general language in 1 John 2:7, 24; 3:11, is telling). There is a division of opinion about how much Paul knew of the Jesus tradition. Many scholars believe that he had almost no knowledge of it, others think he knew only little. I myself am among those who believe he knew several things. He alludes to Jesus' birth and circumcision (Gal 4:4), his suffering, crucifixion, death, burial, resurrection, and appearance to the resurrection witnesses, as well as to specific words of Jesus.[5] However, in his letters he *cites* the concrete Jesus tradition only in a few exceptional cases.

In short, we make the following statement of fact: in the New Testament the concrete Jesus tradition is treated as an *independent entity.* In Acts, the letters, and Revelation it is neither present as quotation nor woven into the fabric of the general proclamation and teaching of Christianity. Again, it *is* present in the Gospels, as it was in the older collections which we may assume lie behind the Gospels, but here again only as an isolated tradition. It is also important to state that the example in Acts 20:35 has the character of a reminder of a word which the church already knew,[6] and that in the two passages in 1 Corinthians Paul expressly says that he had already earlier transmitted to them these two pieces of tradition of which he now must remind them. In 1 Cor 15:3 he writes that this happened *en prōtois,* hence either "among the most important parts" or "at the beginning."[7]

---

[5] Cf. P. Stuhlmacher's two essays in *The Gospel and the Gospels* (n. 1), "The Theme: The Gospel and the Gospels" and "The Pauline Gospel," 1–25 and 149–72 respectively.

[6] The reference to "the words *(tōn logōn)* of the Lord Jesus" can be related to a tract or a category of Jesus tradition. Cf. H. H. Wendt, *Die Apostelgeschichte* (KEK 3; 9th ed.; Göttingen: Vandenhoeck & Ruprecht, 1913), 295.

[7] A more colorless translation of *en prōtois* (e.g., "above all" or "in the first place") is of course possible but does not seem to me likely here. In the solemn style of the pronouncement, where every step is carefully argued, all the main components are certainly accentuated, also *en prōtois.*

When I say that the concrete Jesus tradition is *isolated* I have in mind three things: (1) It is literarily isolated: it only occurs in special documents which probably reflect the existence of a special tradition. (2) The entire tradition assembled in these documents deals with *Jesus:* only he plays a completely independent role in them. No other Jewish teacher or prophet (outside of the scriptures) is allowed to speak here. John the Baptist does play a role but not an independent one. (3) The disciples of Jesus, headed by Peter and the so-called Twelve, are not allowed to supplement Jesus' teaching with positive contributions under their own name. Jesus alone has the floor.[8]

It is clear, however, that the Jesus tradition lies before us *in an edited form.* Jesus' followers have influenced his words in various ways, by interpreting them, explicating them, or undertaking certain alterations of their wording—omissions, additions, and reformulations—and above all when they themselves shaped or reshaped certain narrative traditions. Certain parts—especially the prologues (prehistories, the stories of the baptism and temptation)—seem to be relatively free creations.[9] There is probably also reason to ask whether certain "disciple-works"—logia and parables formulated in the spirit and style of Jesus (cf. Matt 13:51–52)[10]— did not in good faith become a part of the Jesus tradition.

---

[8] On the subject of Jesus as "the only teacher," cf. my contributions *Memory and Manuscript* (n. 2), 332–35; *Tradition and Transmission in Early Christianity* (ConNT 20; Lund: Gleerup, Copenhagen: Munksgaard, 1964, now Stockholm: Almqvist & Wiksell International) 40–44; *The Origins,* sect. 9 (above). Cf. also F. Mussner, "Die Beschränkung auf einen einziger Lehrer," *Israel hat dennoch Gott zum Trost: Festschrift für Schalom Ben-Chorin* (ed. G. Müller; Trier: Paulinus, 1979), 33–43, and R. Riesner, *Jesus als Lehrer: Eine Untersuchung zum Ursprung der Evangelien-Überlieferung* (WUNT² 7; Tübingen: Mohr [Siebeck], 1981; 3d ed., 1988), 37–40. [See now also S. Byrskog, *Jesus the Only Teacher: Didactic Authority and Transmission in Ancient Israel, Ancient Judaism, and the Matthean Community* (ConBNT 24; Stockholm: Almqvist & Wiksell International, 1994).]

[9] Cf. my studies *The Testing of God's Son (Mt 4:1–11 & par.): An Analysis of an Early Christian Midrash* (ConBNT 2:1; Lund: Gleerup, 1966), and "Gottes Sohn als Diener Gottes," *Studia theologica* 27 (1973): 73–106 [now also in the author's *The Shema in the New Testament: Deut 6:4–5 in Significant Passages* (Lund: Novapress, 1996), 139–72].

[10] Cf. my article "The Seven Parables in Matthew XIII," in *New Testament Studies* 19 (1972–73): 33–36 [now also in *The Shema in the New Testament,* 53–74].

II. THE LINK BETWEEN TEXT TYPE
AND "LIFE-SITUATION"

How are we to picture the path of the concrete gospel tradition from Jesus to the evangelists? Since this material is not present in Acts, the letters, or Revelation—neither as completed texts nor as texts in process of formation—and since it is present in the Gospels only as *Jesus* tradition and similarly also in the older collections which shine through the Gospels, the simplest hypothesis is that *throughout the entire period* the concrete Jesus tradition was treated as an isolated tradition. Gerhard Kittel presented this view in a famous statement already in 1926.[11]

This notice, however, was but little observed. At that time the impressive form-critical school had obscured the state of affairs by saying that the isolation is only *a secondary phenomenon*. Both Martin Dibelius and Rudolf Bultmann recognized that in the Gospels the Jesus tradition is present in an isolated form—later Bultmann could refer to Kittel's statement[12]—but they believed that from the beginning it was not so. The evangelists and their predecessors secondarily filtered the Jesus tradition out of primitive Christianity's general preaching, teaching, and other activity for the service of the gospel. They separated the Jesus tradition from a general stream of spiritual material. *From the beginning* the Jesus traditions were restated, shaped and reshaped, and in part freely created, within the various activities of early Christian communities, in typical situations and modes of conduct *(typische Situationen und Verhaltungsweisen)*,[13] and there they

---

[11] "Die *Isolierung* der Jesustradition ist das Konstitutivum des Evangeliums; sie hat aber nie, auch in keinem Stadium der palästinischen Traditionsbildung, gefehlt," in *Die Probleme des palästinischen Spätjudentums und das Urchristentum* (BWANT[3] 1; Stuttgart: Kohlhammer, 1926), 69.

[12] M. Dibelius, *Die Formgeschichte des Evangeliums* (2d ed.; Tübingen: Mohr [Siebeck], 1933), 242–44; ET *From Tradition to Gospel* (trans. B. Lee Wolfe; New York: Scribner's Sons, 1934), 241–43; R. Bultmann, *Die Geschichte der synoptischen Tradition* (2d ed.; FRLANT 29; Göttingen: Vandenhoeck & Ruprecht, 1931), 393–94; ET *The History of the Synoptic Tradition* (trans. J. Marsh; Oxford: Blackwell, 1963; New York: Harper & Row, 1968), 368–69.

[13] Bultmann, *Geschichte*, 4; *History*, 3.

were at home even when people began to bring them together in special collections.

The grounds for this hypothesis are very weak. Our knowledge of the forms of early Christian activity—the typical situations and modes of conduct—is limited: the sources yield only meager information. But what we do know we know from Acts, the letters, and Revelation, and there we find, as we noted earlier, no concrete Jesus traditions at all, neither in a finished form nor in the making.

As a matter of fact the form critics did not derive their hypothesis directly from Acts, the letters, and Revelation, but they based themselves on the view of certain students of general folklore concerning how popular tradition arises in the life of a people in "typical situations and modes of conduct" as spiritual material *(geistiges Gut)* and objectifies itself in typical text-forms *(Gattungen)* before it is eventually written down in various kinds of popular literature *(Kleinliteratur).*[14]

One thing that is impressive in the total view of the form-critical school, as is well known, is the close link drawn between the origin of the gospel materials and the origin and development of early

---

[14] For critical evaluations of form-critical methods, cf. H. Riesenfeld, *The Gospel Tradition and Its Beginnings: A Study in the Limits of "Formgeschichte"* (London: Mowbray, 1957); also in *The Gospel Tradition* (Philadelphia: Fortress, 1970), 1–29; K. Haaker, *Neutestamentliche Wissenschaft: Eine Einführung in Fragestellungen und Methoden* (Wuppertal: Brockhaus, 1981), 48–63; and R. Blank, *Analyse und Kritik der formgeschichtlichen Arbeiten von Martin Dibelius und Rudolf Bultmann* (TD 16; Basel: Reinhardt, 1981). For a detailed analysis of the tendencies in the development of tradition cf. E. P. Sanders, *The Tendencies of the Synoptic Tradition* (SNTSMS 9; Cambridge: Cambridge University Press, 1969). It is interesting to note that the old objections against form criticism which were raised by critics standing outside of the form-critical approach ever since the 1920s, but which were essentially ignored by the representatives of the form-critical school, are now being brought forward even by so pronounced a Bultmann disciple as W. Schmithals, "Kritik der Formkritik," *Zeitschrift für Theologie und Kirche* 77 (1980): 149–85. The argumentation which Schmithals attributes to me in n. 148 is one that I have never used. On the contrary, I have always emphasized that the early Christian traditionists were neither stupid nor ignorant, but men who occupied authoritative positions in the churches; cf. *Tradition,* 25–26; *The Origins,* sect. 5–6 (above).

Christianity itself. The rise and growth of the church, the religious and theological development as well as the formation of texts, belong together. Form critics point to the fact that the text-forms of the gospel material are not merely external style forms: the style is "a sociological reality."[15] Accordingly, the various forms of activity of early Christianity produced the different types *(Gattungen)* of text. And the form of these texts is so distinct and adequate that by them one can tell what function they served and in what life situation *(Sitz im Leben)* they originated.

This hypothesis would have been more illuminating if early Christianity had been a very primitive and exceptionally original movement, one that was uninfluenced by existing culture and forms of activity and by available text models. But that was not the case. All the forms of the activity of early Christianity were already established: preaching, prophecy, admonition, instruction, studies of the scriptures, interpretive discussions, worship services, holy meals, community organization, community discipline, etc. And all the early Christian text categories were of an adopted and traditional nature, except for the synthetically written gospel,[16] which came into being only gradually.

A decisive fact is that the different categories of text present in the Jesus tradition are antecedent to Jesus and early Christianity as *literary* models. One familiar with the holy scriptures and with the preaching and instruction in the synagogues did not first have to place himself in a certain situation, or participate in a certain mode of conduct, in order to formulate a text according to an established literary model. He could freely formulate a text, at his writing desk or wherever, without being bound by the way in which the selected text-form may have arisen originally. The form-critical hypothesis that the form of the Jesus tradition reflects a *Sitz im Leben* which shaped it is not only unproven but also improbable and unnecessary.

---

[15] K. L. Schmidt, "Formgeschichte," *Die Religion in Geschichte und Gegenwart,* 2d ed., 2 (1928), 639, approvingly cited by Dibelius, *From Tradition to Gospel,* 7; cf. Bultmann: "ein soziologischer Begriff, nicht ein ästhetischer" (*Geschichte,* 4); "a sociological concept and not an aesthetic one" (*History,* 4).

[16] Cf. R. Guelich's essay "The Gospel Genre," in *The Gospel and the Gospels* (n. 1), 173–208.

It is further of extraordinary importance to observe that the Jews of the New Testament period had no problem utilizing a variety of textual categories side by side. In the Old Testament it is properly speaking only the Psalms and Proverbs which exhibit only one single genre. In the remaining books a variety of text types appear side by side without difficulty. The same is true of the ancient oral collections of traditional material with which we are familiar, to some extent even of the Mishnah! The genres occur side by side and may also form innumerable hybrids. This too shows how far removed from reality the hypothesis is that the different kinds of texts in the Gospels are always rooted in specific life situations.

III. WHERE WAS PRECISE
TEXT-PRESERVATION NEEDED?

The suspicion that text transmission was perhaps an *independent* act first came to me when I worked with the letter of James, the best example we have of early Christian parenesis. We notice there how the author exhorts with conventional language, yet speaks in his own name. He spontaneously takes his motifs, phrases, and words from the Jesus tradition and the rest of the early Christian tradition (with its rich borrowings from the Jewish and Hellenistic traditions of parenesis). But he does not quote. Even quotations from scripture occur sparingly and are usually only fragmentary. The same is true of the other parenetic passages in the New Testament. Hence the thesis of Dibelius[17] that the words of Jesus were preserved within the framework of early Christian parenesis is not supported by the evidence.

It is especially important, generally speaking, to raise the following question: Where in the operational sphere of early Christianity did people use *texts proper*—logia, parables, narratives, and the like—which were recited as complete units and not just used as a final court of appeal or fragmentarily?[18] Only three particular contexts come to mind.

---

[17] *From Tradition to Gospel,* 233–65.

[18] By a "text" I here mean a self-contained independent utterance— oral or written—in which not only the content but also the form has intrinsic value.

First, we can imagine that people found it natural to recite Jesus texts *in the worship services*. The pericope concerning the Lord's Supper was probably used at sacred meals. Possibly, the oldest form of the passion history was utilized as well (cf. 1 Cor 11:26). People probably also deemed it appropriate to recite in worship other pericopes about Jesus as ready-made, self-contained texts on the model of the synagogue readings from the law and the prophets, but now from memory, not as a lesson from a book.[19]

Second, it is also possible that certain memorized Jesus texts—logia first of all—were employed *in the catechetical instruction* of the early church, even though this cannot be easily documented.

Third, I believe that there existed *a regular study* of the words of Jesus and the stories of his actions and his fate in early Christianity—a study in groups or alone—a Christian form of the pious and learned Jewish Torah studies. In early Christianity communities believers were "occupied (Hebr. *'āsaq*) with" the holy scriptures in their own right in order to participate in divine revelation, which was profitable for wisdom, "for consolation, for teaching, for reproof, for correction, and for training in righteousness" (2 Tim 3:16). It is not hard to imagine that in this study people also used Jesus texts, examined *(eraunan, anakrinein)*[20] them in isolation or in smaller or larger collections.

---

[19] From Riesenfeld's brief presentation in *The Gospel Tradition and Its Beginnings* (n. 14) one gets the impression that in his opinion recitation in the worship services was the fundamental *Sitz im Leben* of the Jesus tradition; see esp. 22–30. In *Memory* (n. 2), I expressed the opinion that early Christianity "worked with the word of the Lord," i.e., the holy scriptures and the Jesus tradition (cf. following note), and that the proper *transmission* of texts occurred within that work but independently, by acts which for the sake of clarity must be separated from the many practical *uses* of the transmitted texts. As one form of *use* among others I mentioned recitation in a worship setting as just a possibility ("not impossible"), 324–35, esp. 335.

[20] Cf., e.g., how the Bereans worked with the scriptures (Acts 17:10–11). On the issue of how we should picture the various forms of "working with the word" in early Christianity, see *Memory,* 191–335; cf. *Tradition* (n. 8), 40. Unfortunately in this essay I cannot develop this subject. See, however, O. Betz, "Jesus' Gospel of the Kingdom," *The Gospel and the Gospels* (n. 1), 53–74.

For the rest, it is hard to imagine contexts in which *entire texts* were used. We can see how the Jesus texts were used in the New Testament by Paul, for instance. Only in two instances does he cite an entire text or a large segment of a text. In other places where he argues about halakic or other theological questions he can reproduce sayings of Jesus in his own words, summarize them, or refer to a fragment from one of them. I have in mind, for example, 1 Cor 7:10 (the question of divorce); 1 Cor 9:14 (the right of a preacher to material support); and 1 Thess 4:15 (the question of the Parousia).[21]

With their dynamic view of the Jesus tradition the form critics could speak of the *Sitz im Leben* of the elements of the tradition and mean by it their point of origin, their use and conservation in the community, their "life situation."[22] One cannot accept such a vague and generalizing hypothesis, however, if one sees that in the Jesus tradition we are dealing with *texts.* Then the following state of affairs emerges: in ever-recurring situations, for example in repeated controversies with outsiders who attacked the teaching or the practice of early Christianity, the churches needed guidelines. However, one did not need a *text* to be read to others. One needed the point of a text, an authoritative teaching from a text, a decisive norm, a convincing argument, the solution to a problem, or something similar. But not necessarily a *text.* When a text was formulated, say a narrative of the type categorized as a dispute *(Streitgespräch),* this certainly did not happen in the situation of controversy itself. And once the text was available as text, people did not use it in controversies as fixed wording to be recited; what they needed was the *content* of the text.

IV. WHAT ABOUT ORAL TEXT-TRANSMISSION?

When in the fifties I became interested in the riddle of the two types of presentation in the New Testament, the Jesus texts plus the free proclamation and teaching about Jesus, I was struck by the fact that in the Jewish material of antiquity there is a corresponding duality. In the targums and especially in the midrashic literature, in the haggadah and other material which somehow ties into the holy

---

[21] *Origins,* sect. 7 (above).
[22] Bultmann, *History,* 11.

scriptures, we see how freely, how imaginatively and creatively the Jewish teachers were able to utilize their sacred texts. Still, despite the long period of this free, creative utilization, the wording of the scriptural texts remained virtually unchanged. The wording was preserved with extraordinary exactness, apart from a few deliberate, minute changes (*tiqqune sopherim* and the like). The question which posed itself was: Where did this precise text-preservation take place and how? Three possible contexts are: (1) The reading of the text in worship services: Here the text was read without any change. (2) The study in the elementary scripture-schools: There the young boys learned to read the text exactly as it stood, without changing it. (3) Absolutely the most important context: There was an intentional and professional practice of text-preservation. Trained writers copied the scriptures and corrected them meticulously in accordance with an original copy. Thus there existed text-preservation and transmission as a practical independent act, not just as an element in the framework of a general use of scripture.[23]

The next question which arose was: How do things stand with regard to oral transmission? In this context we encounter a similar duality: on the one hand there was a rich and flourishing spiritual tradition with free interpretations, vivid variations, creative innovations; but on the other hand there were also units which seemed to be transmitted as fixed texts, not as a common living spiritual tradition.[24]

And how were these texts transmitted? Here too I found that acts of intentional transmission and reception of a fixed text occurred, even when in this case the whole process took place orally. When the teacher passed on such a text he did not necessarily do this with the deeper intent "to console, to teach, to admonish, and to warn" his pupils. Simply to transmit such an important text to a pupil was necessary and valuable in itself. The text might be a point of departure for further teaching on the part of the teacher, for the disciples' own pondering, for a joint exercise in interpretation, or for other practical purposes, but the transmission of the text was an act

---

[23] Cf. *Memory*, 33–70.

[24] The oral texts were, of course, much more diverse than the written ones.

with intrinsic value. Hence there is good reason to make a distinction, even with reference to the oral tradition, between *acts of transmission* as such and the various *uses* which were made of the text transmitted.

Textual transmission could take place in various ways. The teacher might pass on a single text or also a smaller or larger collection of texts. What made the text a fixed one was that the teacher knew it by heart and that the students were also expected to memorize it. It was only by this act that a student could be said to have *received* it and not just *heard* it. The text might also be written down in a notebook, but that did not make much difference. In that case, too, one had to memorize the text; the writing was only an aid to memory, a "memorandum," a *hypomnēma*.[25]

This does not, however, stand in the way of the fact that the text can be *changed*. If he wants to and when he possesses the authority to do it, the teacher can undertake to make a change (or more than one) in a text.[26] But also in this case the pupil receives it in a fixed form, namely in the new wording.

This analysis is the result of the study of *rabbinic* traditions. We have every reason to start there. It is only in this material that we find so many clear pieces of information that we can draw a concrete and explicit picture of how people set about teaching and transmitting the traditional text materials. Once we have a grasp of this process—and I believe that we must have very concrete conceptions of how this proceeded—we can go on to the generally very meager indications we find in other material and ask ourselves if this material was transmitted in a similar manner.[27]

---

[25] With regard to the unofficial written notices, cf. R. O. P. Taylor, *The Groundwork of the Gospel* (Oxford: Blackwell, 1946); *Memory*, 157–63; E. E. Ellis, "New Directions in Form Criticism," 299–315; *The Relationships Among the Gospels: An Interdisciplinary Dialogue* (ed. W. O. Walker Jr.; San Antonio: Trinity University Press, 1978), 123–92; Gerhardsson, *Origins*, sect. 3 (above); Riesner, *Jesus als Lehrer*, 491–98.

[26] Cf. *Memory*, 77–78, 97–98, 103–12, 120–21, 152–53; *Tradition* (n. 8), 38–40. Today I regret that I did not discuss in greater detail the different types of textual changes in the rabbinic writings and the corresponding early Christian material. That would have been worthwhile.

[27] By his form-critical analyses of rabbinic materials, J. Neusner in many respects advanced tradition research. I have in mind particularly *The*

Most of what I sketched of the rabbinic techniques of teaching and transmission reflects the situation in the fully developed rabbinic schools after the fall of the temple in the year 70 and the total destruction of Jerusalem in the year 135. What surfaced was a rather refined technique. Nevertheless, it seemed sensible to make a comparison. For it was clear that in essence the rabbis made use of pedagogical devices that were very ancient. It was not the rabbis who discovered memorization. Nor was it the rabbis who began making a distinction between the inculcation of a text and the interpretation of it. Nor were the rabbis the first to discover that a shorter text is easier to learn than a longer one, that a more vivid and more captivating text is easier to retain than an ordinary flow of words, that rhythmic sentences are not so quickly forgotten as unrhythmic ones, that one should recite in a cantillating way, that people remember things better if they repeat them zealously, etc. Even several of the mnemonic devices of the rabbis are very old.

All this I have laid out in my dissertation *Memory and Manuscript* (1961), adding certain clarifications in the complementary booklet *Tradition and Transmission in Early Christianity* (1964).[28] Many colleagues were pleased with my study, but many have also completely rejected it—with queries, bits of data, individual observations, and all the rest. Sad to say, already at an early stage the debates took an unfortunate turn.[29]

Rabbinic Traditions about the Pharisees before 70 (3 vols.; Leiden: Brill, 1971), and *Early Rabbinic Judaism* (SJLA 13; Leiden: Brill, 1975), 71–136. My main objection to Neusner's picture of the course of tradition is that he has too one-sidedly built it on an analysis of the rabbinic texts without sufficiently taking account of Near Eastern and Hellenistic, Old Testament, and nonrabbinic Jewish materials. Personally I also regret that Neusner does not see anything new in my study *Memory* but speaks of it as a summary of what others have done. Cf. *Exploring the Talmud 1: Education* (ed. H. Z. Dimitrowsky; New York: Ktav, 1976), xxvi–xxvii.

[28] See above nn. 2 and 8.

[29] Often an all too simple picture of my thesis was sketched, which people could then dispatch with equally simple counterarguments. Both kinds of simplification then, partly without further discussion, made their way into the footnotes of handbooks; habent sua fata libelli. With regard to the debates, cf. *Tradition,* in toto; Gerhardsson, *Die Anfänge der Evangelientradition* (GuD 919; Wuppertal: Brockhaus, 1977), 65–69 (bibli-

I have never pictured two four-cornered blocks, one rabbinical and the other early Christian, and said: these two are twins. I have never said that Jesus was only a rabbi, still less that he was a rabbi of the late Tannaitic type; that the disciples formed a rabbinic academy in Jerusalem and that the gospel tradition was a ready-made entity which Jesus drilled into the disciples' memories and which they only had to repeat and to explicate. Nor have I ever said that the Mishnah and the Gospels resembled each other as two eggs in a tray.

What I did say is that Jesus, despite his incomparable grandeur, taught his disciples, and that clearly in traditional style *as far as the external form is concerned.* I have said that his disciples, if in fact they were proper disciples, must have memorized weighty sayings of their master. I have also said that the Twelve, after Jesus' death, probably were for several years residents of Jerusalem and functioned there as an authoritative collegium, and that as such they very likely "worked with the Word of the Lord"—the holy scriptures and the Jesus tradition—in a way basically resembling the "work with the Word" that occurred in other Jewish groups, as for example the leading men of the Qumran community or of the Pharisees.[30]

There is no reason for making a simple block comparison between the fully developed educational system of the rabbis and the activity of Jesus or of early Christianity. Rabbinical forms of instruction, in almost all cases, in instance after instance, are, however, traditional, ancient, and popular. That is what I have maintained all

---

ography); P. H. Davids, "The Gospels and Jewish Tradition: Twenty Years after Gerhardsson," in *Studies of History and Tradition in the Four Gospels* (Gospel Perspectives 1; ed. R. T. France and D. Wenham; Sheffield: JSOT Press, 1980), 75–97; Riesner, *Jesus als Lehrer* (n. 8), passim, esp. 18–79.

[30] Cf. my brief historical sketch in *Memory,* 324–35. Cf. how I present Luke's view of things ("The Witness of Luke," ibid., 208–61) and Paul's view ("The Evidence of Paul," ibid., 262–323). In the ensuing discussion many scholars have obviously confused especially the Lucan perspective with my own. With reference to the debates about the place of Jerusalem in early Christianity, cf. among others B. Holmberg, *Paul and Power: The Structure of Authority in the Primitive Church as Reflected in the Pauline Epistles* (Lund: Gleerup, 1978, and Philadelphia: Fortress, 1980), and J. D. G. Dunn, "The Relationship between Paul and Jerusalem according to Galatians 1 and 2," *New Testament Studies* 28 (1982): 461–78.

the time,[31] and this is now what Rainer Riesner has independently demonstrated with much evidence from pre-Christian sources in his important book *Jesus als Lehrer* (1981).[32]

More use can be made of the comparative material, Jewish as well as Hellenistic, than Riesner, I, and others[33] have made of it. Now already, however, we know enough to take element after element in the practice of the ancient teachers—and also of the prophets; there is no reason to overlook them—and to ask: Was the Jesus tradition transmitted in a similar way? To what extent did Jesus himself and the early Christian authorities practice the ancient forms of oral instruction and oral transmission? Was this the case throughout early Christianity or only in parts of it?[34] Over the whole period or only gradually? I think many problems that were insurmountable until now could be satisfactorily explained if they were viewed in the light of the materials consulted.

One aspect of the subject is that the transmitting *persons* are of interest: Peter, the three pillars, the Twelve, Paul, etc.; and how they were linked with the chain of tradition which glimmers through them. The form critics did not think much of the information which the ancient church provides concerning the concrete persons behind the Gospels, not even of the personal references in the New Testament. The notion of the creative community makes questions of concrete traditionists uninteresting. This depersonalization has had a contagious effect right into the present. It still regularly happens that people blithely speak of "products of the church" *(Gemeindebildungen)* and of traditions which "circulated in the communities," instead of asking *who* has formulated, reformulated, or transmitted a certain text.

---

[31] *Memory,* 24, 76–78; *Tradition,* 13–21; *The Origins,* sect. 3 (above).

[32] Cf. above, n. 8.

[33] Cf., e.g., R. A. Culpepper's presentation of a variety of Hellenistic and Jewish school forms, *The Johannine School: An Evaluation of the Johannine-School Hypothesis Based on an Investigation of the Nature of Ancient Schools* (SBLDS 26; Missoula: Scholars Press, 1975).

[34] Cf., e.g., U. Wilckens's opinion of the double tradition-historical currents of Jesus memories in early Christianity, "Tradition de Jésus et kérygme du Christ: La double histoire de la tradition au sein du Christianisme primitif," *Revue d'histoire et de philosophie religieuses* 47 (1967): 1–20. [See now above all Byrskog, *Jesus the Only Teacher* (n. 8).]

V. THE PATH OF THE SYNOPTIC TRADITION

Let me briefly indicate how I picture the path of the synoptic tradition from Jesus to the evangelists. We may call this approach a working hypothesis. There are two facts one may not lose sight of: (1) That in the eyes of early Christianity Jesus was a unique and incomparable figure, King of kings and Lord of lords; and we may add: Prophet of prophets, Teacher of teachers, Messiah, Son of God, *Kyrios*. No one was considered his equal. (2) That it was not Jesus the wisdom teacher, prophet, or miracle worker who was the center of early Christian convictions, but Jesus the crucified, the risen and living Lord, the exclusive Redeemer and Savior of the world.

Without forgetting these facts we may try to answer a few questions with the help of ordinary historical methods: from a purely technical view, how did Jesus operate when he preached and taught? How were his words received by his disciples and other adherents? How were these words then handed down? How were a number of them provided with a narrative framework? And how did the narrative traditions originate? How did the larger synthetic collections come into being? And so forth.

That Jesus of Nazareth, despite his incomparable majesty, gave instruction is an item of information from the sources which we cannot dismiss as a secondary feature of the tradition.[35] By no means opposed to this is the fact that he also acted as a charismatic and a prophet. As many have noted, there were no clear boundaries between the teacher and the prophet. A teacher could be charismatic, and a prophet could have a didactic disposition. Moreover, both gathered around them disciples who preserved their pronouncements as well as the memory of their acts and fates.[36]

---

[35] Cf. esp. Riesner, *Jesus als Lehrer.*

[36] I do not think that the difference between M. Hengel's and my view of the teacher-charismatic relationship is as great as one would expect from reading Hengel's *Nachfolge und Charisma: Eine exegetisch-religionsgeschichtliche Studie zu Mt 8,21 f. und Jesu Ruf in die Nachfolge* (Berlin: Töpelmann, 1968); ET *The Charismatic Leader and His Followers* (trans. J. C. G. Greig; Edinburgh: T&T Clark, 1981). Cf. idem, "Jesus als messianischer Lehrer der Weisheit und die Anfänge der Christologie," *Sagesse et religion* (Paris: Presse universitaire de France, 1979), 147–88. Cf.

True, Jesus' high self-consciousness, and the exalted image which early Christianity had of him, conferred, in the eyes of his adherents, a special personal value on his utterances and the stories of his deeds. His words and the narratives of episodes in his life were certainly felt as extraordinarily important, even indispensable, so that they were preserved, studied, and examined for their own sake, not only for a variety of practical reasons. Of Jesus' words it was said they were "spirit and life" (John 6:63), that they would never pass away (Matt 24:35), that it was a matter of supreme importance "to hear and to do them" (Matt 7:24–27 and parallels), etc. To me it is impossible to imagine an early Christian leader or teacher who would have been content with a purely mythical picture of Christ. This possibility exists certainly only in the fantasy of some modern exegetes. Riesner puts it very well when he says that Jesus' understanding of himself and the interpretation of Jesus in early Christianity must have been an extraordinary motive for transmission of the tradition.[37]

The early Christian sources show unequivocally that Jesus' adherents were exclusively bound to *Jesus;* none of them was referred to another teacher or prophet for supplementary studies. Jesus was the only master of early Christianity in the sense that he possessed a unique and incomparable, a decisive and permanent authority as representative of God and mediator of a definitive revelation and a decisive work of redemption. The adherents of Jesus were to regard him as "the only teacher," as Matt 23:8 expressly prescribed—regardless of whether the formulation is an element of interpretation or an authentic utterance of Jesus. This attitude is demonstrated above all in the fact that, strictly speaking, the concrete Jesus tradition is only interested in Jesus: there is no other teacher or prophet next to him. Nor did any of his followers receive the role of "successor in office."[38]

---

further the essay "Gospels Criticism: A Perspective on the State of the Art" by E. E. Ellis in *The Gospel and the Gospels* (n. 1) 26–52, esp. 42–43. [See now also Byrskog, *Jesus the Only Teacher* (n. 8), 33–196.]

[37] ". . . ein ausserordentliches Tradierungsmotiv," *Jesus als Lehrer,* 351–52.

[38] Cf. *Origins,* sect. 9 (above) [and now also Byrskog, *Jesus the Only Teacher,* 197–403].

This is true of the entire period beginning with Jesus up to the time of the evangelists. The concrete Jesus tradition possessed a special dignity and was something unique. And it belonged to the foundation which every Christian church had to have. Already at their founding—*en prōtois*—the churches needed the Jesus tradition as much as they needed certain holy scriptures of the old covenant. In none of these instances do the sources inform us how the required texts were passed on. Usually we make only slight (if any) mention of things that are self-evident to us. For that reason it is practically an accident when they appear in a source (cf., e.g., 2 Tim 4:13).

VI. THE SAYINGS TRADITION

For reasons of space I shall here content myself with a simple distinction between a tradition of sayings and a tradition of narratives. I assume the detailed divisions are familiar enough.

With regard to the *sayings tradition,* it is striking that Jesus' words—logia as well as parables—are artful texts, formed with care and bearing all the marks of poetic and narrative-technical skill.[39] Here we are not dealing with ordinary everyday utterances, or simple informative, descriptive, and prescriptive sentences. Nor is it just we who view matters this way; the evangelists were also conscious of this. To Jesus' words—logia as well as parables—they give an appellation: *parabolai,* which corresponds to the Hebrew *meshālim.*[40] A *māshāl* is a short, artful utterance; by contrast with everyday speech it is an artistically formulated little text.

What distinguishes this sort of statement from ordinary utterances is that not only the content but also the form and wording themselves have intrinsic value. Not only does the speaker wish to communicate something to his hearers, but he objectivizes it, creates an object which he "passes on" to them: the text. This object or text

---

[39] Cf. Riesner, *Jesus als Lehrer,* 392–407.

[40] Cf. Joachim Jeremias, *Die Gleichnisse Jesu* (7th ed.; Berlin: Evangelische Verlagsanstalt, 1972), 16; ET *The Parables of Jesus* (trans. S. H. Hooke; rev. ed.; New York: Scribner's Sons, 1963), 17 [and now also my "The Narrative Meshalim in the Synoptic Gospels," *New Testament Studies* 34 (1988): 339–42].

is not conceived as worthless wrapping paper that can immediately be disposed of. It is intended to be preserved.

It is true of many logia and parables of Jesus that they are not intended simply to give information or to prescribe something but *to open the eyes of the listeners;* their purpose is to lead the listeners to see something and to assent to it. But the text is also given to be kept and so to enable people to preserve, renew, broaden, and deepen the insight and, not least of all, to enable them to pass it on. To receive a mashal is to acquire not only an insight but also the medium by which one can preserve and spread the insight.

To a great extent this observation proves to be true both with regard to the parables and to the short logia.[41] After all, as a rule there is less room for variation in the wording of a short logion than in a narrative parable. In the case of the latter, one is tempted to make it either as "literary" as possible or to change it at certain points to indicate discoveries one believes one has made in the parable. This we notice when we compare the synoptic parallels. One can also tell this from the way it is clothed in Greek. As a rule the logia are closer to the Aramaic than are the parables.[42]

For the form critics it was quite natural to think that numerous Jewish wisdom utterances and early Christian words of prophecy were, as the tradition was transmitted, put on the lips of the earthly Jesus. I reckon with the possibility that this may have happened—in good faith—but hardly without further ado or frequently. The attitude toward the Jesus texts, and the fact that they are not all that numerous,[43] have helped to make it easy to distinguish them from other material. For this reason it certainly has captured public attention when a hitherto unknown saying of Jesus surfaced. F. Neugebauer,

---

[41] See previous note and cf. Riesner, *Jesus als Lehrer,* 392–404.

[42] Cf. M. Black, *An Aramaic Approach to the Gospels and Acts* (3d ed.; Oxford: Clarendon, 1967; repr. Peabody, Mass.: Hendrickson, 1998), 274–77.

[43] We usually postulate that the evangelists made a scant selection from an abundant stream of Jesus tradition. One must remember, however, that the extant extracanonical tradition does not support the postulate that the Jesus tradition was rich. (The gnostic and gnosticizing gospels do not even pretend to transmit sayings of the earthly Jesus; they present secret words of the risen or ascended Lord.) Cf. the essay "Unknown Sayings of Jesus" by O. Hofius, *The Gospel and the Gospels* (n. 1), 336–60.

D. Hill, and J. D. G. Dunn have raised weighty objections against the opinion of the form critics that Jewish wisdom sayings and especially early Christian words of prophecy were simply put on the lips of the earthly Jesus.[44] I believe that this could happen from time to time but then in good faith and not without testing.[45]

It is also clear that sayings of Jesus have changed on their way from Jesus to the evangelists. Our texts reveal errors in memory, variations in translation, interpretive adaptations, and the like. Formulations are omitted, added, changed, etc. Occasionally this may have happened in a more charismatic-prophetic way, and at other times in a more rational-didactic manner, the latter being the more frequent. By this process later, postresurrection issues, ideas, and perspectives were embedded in the sayings of Jesus. One must remember, however, that as a rule this apparently occurred only to a limited extent. When, for example, we consider the sayings of Jesus in the so-called Q material, we are struck by how little they have been influenced by the passion and resurrection stories of early Christianity or even by post-Easter Christology, soteriology, pneumatology, and eschatology.

This is notable, since it is hard to believe that there was even a single early Christian community which was not interested in Jesus' death and resurrection or the redemptive-historical significance of these crucial events. The Q material can never have expressed "the whole truth," all that the circle behind it believed, thought, and taught about Jesus. For my part I believe—partly in agreement with A. Polag—that the "archaic" character of the logia and parables of Jesus is most easily explained as a pointer to the circumstance that they were transmitted in fixed wording and with minimal editing

---

[44] F. Neugebauer, "Geistsprüche und Jesuslogien," *Zeitschrift für die Neutestamentliche Wissenschaft* 53 (1962): 218–28; D. Hill, "On the Evidence for the Creative Role of Christian Prophets," *ibidem* 20 (1973–74): 262–74; J. D. G. Dunn, "Prophetic 'I'-sayings and the Jesus-tradition: The Importance of Testing Prophetic Utterances within Early Christianity," *ibidem* 24 (1977–78): 175–98. The problem is further discussed in M. E. Boring, *Sayings of the Risen Jesus: Christian Prophecy and the Synoptic Tradition* (SNTSMS 46; Cambridge: Cambridge University Press, 1982) [and now also D. E. Aune, *Prophecy in Early Christianity and the Ancient Mediterrranean World* (Grand Rapids: Eerdmans, 1983), 233–45].

[45] Cf. the reference in n. 10 above.

from the time before Easter onward.[46] Nor is it only in the Q material that we can see how little the Christology of the church was allowed to change the sayings of Jesus. This is, above all, characteristic of all the parables. (There are of course exceptions, especially in the case of interpretive additions.)[47]

VII. THE NARRATIVE TRADITION

As far as the *narrative traditions* are concerned, these, as we all know, have certain peculiarities. Dibelius felt impelled to say that the tradition of narrative and the tradition of sayings were not subject to the same law.[48]

The principal difference between the tradition of sayings and the tradition of narrative actually consists in the fact that the sayings have in principle an articulated form *even from the beginning*, the form they had when first spoken. The tradition of narrative on the other hand must have been formulated by someone who either saw or heard of what happened; hence the text originated at one or several steps' remove from the principal figure.

But of the narrative traditions we also can see that the sayings of Jesus in them have been subjected to less editing than the narrative elements in these texts. Here, too, respect for the exact wording of the sayings asserts itself. Greater freedom to edit the narrative elements and so to restructure the tradition of narrative as a whole or to rebuild the whole narrative in a new way has furthermore brought with it the possibility that it could be more easily influenced by the kerygma and the post-Easter outlook of early Christianity than the sayings within the narratives.

---

[46] A. Polag, *Die Christologie der Logienquelle* (WMANT 45; Neukirchen-Vluyn: Neukirchener Verlag, 1977), 143. Cf. Polag's essay "The Theological Center of the Sayings Source," *The Gospel and the Gospels* (n. 1), 97–105.

[47] Cf. A. Polag, *Christologie,* passim. [See now also my article "The Earthly Jesus in the Synoptic Parables," *Christology, Controversy, and Community: New Testament Essays in Honour of David R. Catchpole* (ed. D. G. Horrell and C. M. Tuckett; NTSup 99; Leiden: Brill, 2000), 49–62.]

[48] *From Tradition to Gospel* (n. 12), 28.

I do not believe, however, that this must be understood as though the narrative elements or traditions had a fluid wording. Once a narrative text was formulated, it, too, was handed down in memorized form, possibly with written notes for support. We must in the first place reckon with the fact that the changes we discover were *deliberate* changes, introduced by authoritative teachers or authors for the purpose of making clear a certain meaning.

It is not necessary in this brief sketch to discuss all the types of narrative text we can distinguish in the synoptic material. On the whole it is not very important to distinguish these materials, when one considers them as only different literary patterns which one can make use of without being occupied in some specific *Sitz im Leben*. There is no reason, as we have said, to presume that the narrative Jesus traditions originated as texts in various "situations and modes of conduct." They were certainly formulated on the basis of conscious editorial work. Apart from a category of vigorously inspired sayings, a text is normally formulated *deliberately* and that by an individual person.[49] This person may perform the task in a private context or in a study group assembled for this purpose, regardless of what text model he has adopted.

In this connection the group certainly played a stimulating role—asking questions and answering them, wondering and discussing—but also functioned as an instrument of social control. One must assume that without the consent of this group no new text or variegated form of a text could be accepted and spread.

In the formulation of certain types of text—I have in mind particularly the so-called pronouncement stories[50]—the framework may have been formed rather freely. I believe, however, that even

---

[49] Among the various forms of text production in the nations of the world (cf. n. 56) there are of course also examples of how a text comes into being as different listeners influence, with their own verbal participation, the forward movement of a storyteller; see, e.g., *Tro, sanning, sägen: Tre bidrag till en folkloristisk metodik* (ed. B. af Klintberg; Stockholm: Norstedt, 1973), 95–101.

[50] Cf. *Semeia* 20 (1981), *Pronouncement Stories,* ed. R. C. Tannehill. The fact that these kinds of text were of Hellenistic origin is no hindrance to their being a familiar literary text pattern in Palestine before the beginning of the Christian era.

these kinds of text were normally formed in connection with transmitted sayings of Jesus. Also the texts conveying didactic or polemical dialogues may well have a decisive saying of Jesus as their historical nucleus. And in this instance it is not at all impossible that the frame story, in all its brevity, can also proceed from a factual event.[51]

As far as the passion stories are concerned, we there encounter the peculiar circumstance that although they consist of small self-contained units they are more firmly connected with each other and refer to each other to a greater extent than do the other pericopes. From this circumstance the form critics derived the insight that the passion story in its basic form emerged early as a coherent whole.[52] Rudolf Pesch believes that the narrative sequence in Mark 8–16 concerning Jesus' journey through Caesarea Philippi to Jerusalem and the events which occurred there, at a very early stage (before A.D. 37) formed a primitive gospel, indeed in the infant church in Jerusalem.[53] I am fairly receptive to Pesch's proposals for reconstruction even though many of the details will have to remain uncertain.

VIII. CRITICAL POINTS FOR FORM CRITICISM

Before I conclude I wish briefly, in part as a summary and in part as an expansion, to list and comment on ten critical points for classical form criticism:

(1) The distinction between "Palestinian" and "Hellenistic." In the face of what we know today about the strong Hellenistic influence in Palestine we can use this distinction for making historical

---

[51] To the extent that one may take account of the fact that the tradition was subject to "control," the narrative frameworks gain an a priori higher value as sources.

[52] Dibelius, *From Tradition to Gospel* (n. 12), 178–217; Bultmann, *The History* (n. 12), 275. On this cf. Blank, *Analyse und Kritik* (n. 14), 52–55, 151–55. For my part, I think the passion narrative started as early Christianity's answer to the official death sentence upon Jesus.

[53] R. Pesch, *Das Evangelium der Urgemeinde: Wiederhergestellt und erläutert* (Freiburg: Herder, 1979); for the details, see Pesch's large commentary on Mark. Cf. further his response to criticism in his essay in *The Gospel and the Gospels* (n. 1), 106–48.

judgments only in exceptional cases. An important instrument of differentiation in the arsenal of the form critics has therefore come to nothing.

(2) The idea that a synoptic text form *(Gattung)* should be viewed as "a sociological fact." Even before the time of Jesus and early Christianity, these various forms existed as literary patterns which were utilized side by side in the same context. There is no necessary connection between a conventional textual model and a specific situation or activity.

(3) The link between text form and *Sitz im Leben*. If one should ask where a given synoptic text took shape the correct answer is not: in the "life situation" where it was most urgently needed. The text was certainly formulated in the course of deliberate textual labor. In light of this insight an additional aid has become useless.

(4) The search for the pure form. The fact that there are so few texts in the Synoptic Gospels which meet the requirements of pure form, in conjunction with the fact that mixed textual types were already current in pre-Christian materials, makes this search pointless. It only tempts us to make unhistorical generalizations.

(5) "Unliterary" and "literary." Neither Jesus nor the Twelve nor other influential teachers of early Christianity were "unliterary" people to whom texts, oral transmission of fixed forms, or copying were foreign. From ancient times on, such matters were well known in Israel, indeed everyday actions in the life of society. Prophets appeared on the scene and passed their words on to disciples who received them, transmitted them by word of mouth, or wrote them down. In the course of time books of prophecy were compiled. Wisdom teachers appeared and their disciples acted in the same way. In the course of time books of wisdom were compiled. Neither Jesus nor early Christianity needed to invent such skills or introduce them as innovations. The direct textual labor which the evangelists performed was no more than a refined form of the deliberate textual labor which was customary among Jesus' followers even from the time of Jesus' activity on earth, and which Jesus himself also practiced in his own way when he carefully formulated his logia and parables.

(6) The relation between tradition and redaction. When one remembers that throughout the whole period the concrete Jesus

tradition consisted essentially of *texts* that were memorized, interpreted, compiled, grouped, and regrouped and on which authoritative teachers could undertake certain redactional operations (particularly in connecting elements but also in the text of the traditions), then another picture emerges, one that differs from the
scheme "first tradition—then redaction." The situation was much
more one of continual interplay between transmission and redaction. As far as redactional operations are concerned, they need not
have been totally unhistorical. Such changes could also be made
with knowledge of historical realities.

(7) The independence of individual traditions. In all likelihood
the sayings of Jesus were originally independent of each other and in
the course of time only to a limited extent reworked and adapted to
the rest of the material. The fictive speeches in the Synoptic Gospels
retain the character of mosaics.[54] Concerning the narrative traditions
one must assume, on the other hand, that both the person who first
formulated such texts and those who later worked on them had a
total image of Jesus which influenced their formulations. Hence the
individual narrative tradition must not be regarded as completely
independent texts to the same degree as the logia and the parables.

(8) The traditionists. On the basis of their view as to how popular tradition came into being, the form critics were hardly interested
in the persons behind the synoptic texts. But in several respects this
matter is important. Where tradition is controlled and cultivated,
the bearers are important. In all likelihood the early church arose
around the circle of Jesus' closest disciples and it is equally probable
that from the beginning they had learned the logia and parables by
heart. Besides, Jesus' works and fate were still fresh in their minds.
Thus the gospel tradition begins with certain traditionists who were
well versed in the history of Jesus; and from the beginning it consists
of a large number of loose logia and parables from the lips of Jesus as

---

[54] It seems to me that in the present situation it is difficult to decide
the extent to which the larger text structures ("midrashic patterns") found
in the discourses of the Gospels, could possibly go back to Jesus himself (cf.
Ellis, "New Directions in Form Criticism" [n. 25], 309–15, and his essay
"Gospel Criticism: A Perspective on the State of the Art," *The Gospel and
the Gospels,* esp. 42–43). We still know too little of the different forms of
"work with the word" in early Christianity.

well as of recollections of weighty episodes in his work—memories which had not yet crystallized into texts.

(9) The relationship between oral and written tradition. Before Matthew and Luke the gospel traditions were not available in a published (book) form. It is hardly to be believed that the Gospel of Mark was intended to be a written summary of the entire Jesus tradition. Written records of varying length, like notes and memory aids *(hypomnēmata),*[55] were surely in circulation at a very early stage. It is not impossible, though perhaps not likely, that such records were kept by the disciples and others already in the period of Jesus' activity. In any case, they may well have come into use rather rapidly in the early church, especially in predominantly Hellenistic-influenced congregations. I, for my part, believe that such records were only intended to be used as memory aids since the synoptic texts were in principle oral texts. It is, at any rate, hard to tell from looking at a text whether it was formulated only to serve the memory or also to be recorded on a sheet of papyrus. I know of no one who has provided us with stable criteria for judging this so far. Written texts may be firmly fixed; they may also be changeable. Oral texts may be changeable but also stable—extraordinarily stable even. It is not at all easy to attain certainty on this point: penetrating research and discussion are still needed.[56]

(10) Mark's achievement. If Mark wrote the first of the Gospels preserved for us,[57] this hardly constituted a radically new beginning. Even before him thorough textual work was done in the church and compilations of varying lengths of Jesus traditions had been made.

---

[55] Cf. the literature mentioned in n. 25 above.

[56] If one remembers that even within a single culture oral tradition can be very diverse, and that it is inexhaustibly diverse when one includes all cultures in one's purview, it seems important to try to establish which analogies to the Jesus tradition seem nearest to it. It is not clear to me, for instance, why we should elevate the type which A. B. Lord investigated in Yugoslavia to the status of standard model for "orality," "oral tradition," "oral composition," "oral literature," or the like, when after all the world is full of alternatives. Cf. the discussion of Lord's theories in *The Relationships among the Gospels* (n. 25), 31–122. The phenomenon "written tradition" is also a variegated entity.

[57] The arguments recently adduced against the priority of Mark's Gospel have not convinced me so far.

The narrative of Jesus' passion, death, and resurrection was certainly created very early and it cried out for an introduction. The rough plan which Mark followed in part came about quite naturally: a simple geographic-chronological sketch (starting with John the Baptist, followed by the main ministry in Galilee and concluding with a final journey to Jerusalem, with the events there recorded in a natural order), united with the knowledge that Jesus busied himself in the main with preaching, teaching, exorcizing demons, and healing the sick. The integrative identification of Jesus and the consideration of his work as a whole that Mark offers were found not only in the kerygma but also in comprehensive surveys of Jesus' ministry as we encounter them, for instance, in the speeches in Acts and in the formalized Christological material.

IX. A SOUND STARTING POINT

When the New Testament writings were assembled it seemed natural to distinguish between *Euangelion* (writings containing concrete Jesus material) and *Apostolos* (writings containing unconstrained apostolic instruction). Never mind that these designations might occasion misunderstanding: the apostles had had to deal with the gospel material, and their own free instruction contained also the good news about Jesus Christ. Yet, viewed objectively, there is justification for this division (with a certain reservation, of course, as it pertains to John's Gospel). There is also justification for placing the *Euangelion* first and treating these texts as basic. This does not have to eclipse the kerygma.

What the form critics did was to incorporate the *Euangelion* in the *Apostolos*. According to them the Gospels and the tradition underlying them should in principle be viewed as post-Easter proclamation of the church concerning Christ. This means that, on the question of historicity, the criteria have been reversed: the burden of proof no longer rests with the person who regards a given Jesus tradition as unauthentic but with the person who asserts its authenticity.

It cannot be correct for us as historians to accept this point of departure. Historians have to take seriously the clear distinction that the early Christian sources make—with the exception of John's Gospel. Our starting point has to be the assertion of the sources that

Jesus said and did what they say he said and did. I say this has to be our *point of departure*. As scholarly investigators employing histori-cal-critical methods we must, of course, test the isolated units as well as the larger complexes in terms of these questions: Can this or that really have been said or done by Jesus? Can this really have happened to him? Does this text in its present form or in some earlier form yield reliable information? Hence the burden of proof must lie on our shoulders when we doubt the assertions of the sources and sepa-rate out secondary material. Moreover, a memento has been fur-nished us by the debates about the question of basic criteria: to all appearances it hardly leads to a single undisputed result.[58]

Our criticism is necessary because we know—better than the church before us knew—that the Jesus traditions have been edited before they were written down. From that perspective it is necessary to examine what are probably post-Easter interpretations, changes, additions, or secondary creations. A number of texts in the Gospels are obviously rather free interpretive creations. I have in mind above all the prologues: the prehistories in Matthew and Luke as well as the narratives of the baptism and temptation of Jesus. But here, too, I believe that early Christianity took its starting point in something handed down, and, in the final analysis, something historical. Briefly expressed: *it only gave an interpretation where there was some-thing to be interpreted.* This simple rule of thumb may also be applied in the evaluation of John's Gospel.

In short, I would by no means plead for a narrow-minded bibli-cism or a general credulity with regard to the assertions of the New Testament documents. In his or her analysis the investigator must be keen, unbiased, and thorough; in the search for truth relentless criti-cism is indispensable.

One must, however, have a sound starting point.

---

[58] For a balanced discussion of the various criteria, cf. R. H. Stein, "The 'Criteria' for Authenticity," *Studies of History and Tradition* (n. 29), 225–63.

III

The Gospel Tradition

INTRODUCTION

Our word "tradition" covers a basic and omnipresent—but also complex and elusive—feature of human existence. Scholars in many disciplines study it, but we still look in vain for works which combine insights from all the pertinent disciplines into a comprehensive and synthetic description of the phenomenology of tradition.[1]

Historically, Christianity may be characterized as a new tradition which originates within a well-developed mother-tradition from which it gradually liberates itself; at the same time it also receives influences from other traditions in the milieu. This essay deals with the gospel tradition, seen as part of the early Christian tradition. Let me indicate the way I delimit my subject. Certainly I am going to mobilize insights from many areas and many disciplines, but the historical sphere we shall directly deal with is early Christianity in the New Testament period against its background in the Judaism of the centuries around the beginning of our era and in its "Hellenistic" surroundings. Within this area we shall study tradition in its most important aspects, especially the gospel tradition. With

---

[1] Cf. however, P.-G. Müller, *Der Traditionsprozess im Neuen Testament: Kommunikationsanalytische Studien zur Versprachlichung des Jesusphänomens* (Freiburg, Basel, Wien: Herder, 1982), II–III, and E. Shils, *Tradition* (London: Faber & Faber, 1981). For literature on the gospel tradition, see R. Riesner, *Jesus als Lehrer: Eine Untersuchung zum Ursprung der Evangelien-Überlieferung* (WUNT² 7; Tübingen: Mohr [Siebeck], 1981; 2d ed., 1984), 503–68, 615.

the last designation—as well as with the phrase "the concrete Jesus tradition"—I mean the tradition about the teaching, work, and fate of Jesus during his life on earth (including the signs of his resurrection), *in concreto,* mainly tradition of the sort which has been compiled in the Synoptic Gospels (and in a more elaborate form in the Gospel of John).

We may analyze and discuss early Christian (and Jewish) tradition with the aid of a rather simple model of investigation which I will soon present. But let me first say that I am aware that further distinctions and classifications are possible and desirable; however, such specifications belong to more penetrating analysis and specialized debate. I also know that my terminology is somewhat rough. It is, however, useful, and that is important even in scholarly discussions. Finally, I also know that my distinctions sometimes appear artificial, since tradition in its best stages is a rather well integrated, organically coherent entity. Yet, I intend my distinctions to be realistic: very commonly the different aspects of tradition are disjoined and the different elements exist separately. We do need a convenient term for each one of them.

One of my purposes is to emphasize questions where further research and discussion are desirable. I shall mention here a very great number of such questions, old and new, and put a special stress on some of them. The answers I sketch very briefly are primarily meant as illustrations of the model of investigation and of the problems; as solutions of complicated problems they are rather approximate and preliminary.

I am a Christian, brought up in the Lutheran tradition. Certain proclivities and accents will presumably reveal that. But in no way do I reject different attempts to clarify the early Christian tradition from confessional points of departure. In his book *Der Traditionsprozess im Neuen Testament* (1981), Paul-Gerhard Müller has made an insightful and many-sided analysis of the (verbal) New Testament tradition from a Catholic standpoint. Similar works ought to be done from non-Catholic positions as well. However, the approach I present here is not founded on any specific theological basis. Apart from certain brief digressions and asides, I here tackle the problem of tradition by means of secular scholarship. While this facilitates discussion with nontheological disciplines, I want to point out, on the other hand, that my approach should not be naively developed into a New Testament theology. In a *historical* study of the origin and first development of Christianity one must consider the earthbound human reality with its whole mixture of conflicting elements, shortcomings, compromises, and the like. If, on the other hand, a *New Testament theology* is to give a fresh picture of early Christianity's message and content of faith, it cannot begin in the outer, earthly dimensions but must take the eruptive center of the message itself, as its starting point, i.e., those convictions, views, and perspectives that animated Jesus and his followers and created early Christianity—the reign of heaven, Christ, the gospel—as preached and believed.

I. A MODEL OF INVESTIGATION

It is my conviction that historical research must try to make very concrete reconstructions of the past, preferably in the form of vivid, visual pictures of the complex realities. The sources do not always allow that. But we can often advance rather far in the right direction if we apply, on the one hand, general ("phenomenological") insights about the way in which human beings function both individually and communally, and, on the other hand, special insights from that historical sphere in which the object of research is situated and from the analogies closest to it.

For the study of the early Christian tradition we need a model of investigation. I have used one such model (with increasing clearness) in my works on the problem of tradition.[2] This model makes it possible to dissect the complicated phenomenon of early Christian

---

[2] *Memory and Manuscript: Oral Tradition and Written Transmission in Rabbinic Judaism and Early Christianity* (ASNU 22; Lund: Gleerup, Copenhagen: Munksgaard, 1961); *Tradition and Transmission in Early Christianity* (ConNT 20; Lund: Gleerup, Copenhagen: Munksgaard, 1964) [repr. in one volume, Grand Rapids: Eerdmans; Livonia: Dove, 1999)]; *The Origins of the Gospel Tradition* (see above); *The Path of the Gospel Tradition* (see above). In the following I will make frequent reference to these writings in order to indicate the continuity and development of my work on the problem of tradition, in the hope of eliminating misunderstandings of my position.

tradition, to elucidate its different aspects in congruent ways, to keep in mind the most important of them in the analyses of the texts, and to discuss the problems involved.

The model is based on general phenomenological insights gained in many areas, times, and disciplines, but it is specifically constructed for a study of *the early Christian tradition* connected with its historical milieus, especially its *Jewish mother-tradition.* I shall here present it briefly yet in a more developed and explicated way than I have done before.[3] The model is simple: a basic distinction is made between inner and outer tradition, and, within the outer tradition four separate aspects are to be noted: verbal, behavioral, institutional, and material tradition.

In the following I first present the model of investigation in general phenomenological terms and then show more concretely what it means when applied to the mother-tradition of Christianity and to early Christianity itself. Then I discuss the different aspects in somewhat more detail in relation to early Christianity. The main stress will be laid upon the gospel tradition.

1. Survey: Inner and Outer Tradition

Inner tradition. When tradition functions ideally, it is animated, it "lives." It is carried and kept together by an inner engagement, by belief, convictions, values, views. An ideal traditionist is like a torch that lights other torches, some rabbis used to say.

The fundamental convictions and intentions of a human being cannot remain locked up in the individual. They express themselves in the fellowship, they become messages which are communicated to other people, they spread to the environment and to the next generation, if they are strong. They generate tradition. The decisive, "living" part of this, however, is difficult to analyze and describe. The words we use to indicate that one human being influences others are rather vague. We say that he inspires others, convinces others, dominates others, is contagious and so on. This is a kind of communication—a handing over and a receiving; therefore the word "tradition"

---

[3] Cf. *Memory,* 71–78, 290–94; *Tradition,* 7; *Origins,* sects. 1 and 4 (above).

is appropriate: "inner tradition." It is of course necessary to study the inner tradition but it is not easy. As an object of research it is elusive and difficult to grasp as is life itself: it changes and varies, some parts grow, other parts decline, renewal occurs, and it can die. An analysis—which I am not going to do here—would have to include many aspects: cognitive, emotive, and volitional aspects, perhaps more.

What is easier to come to grips with is the outward forms the inner tradition assumes. It not only expresses itself in a mental way, it also *externalizes* itself in visible and audible outward forms. These I call outer tradition.

Outer tradition. The outward forms of a tradition can be of many kinds. For our purpose it seems sufficient to specify four such forms or dimensions:

(1) Verbal tradition (word-tradition). Inner tradition finds non-verbal expression in inarticulate sounds, glances, mimicry, head movements, gestures with the hands, pointing and signing with the fingers, and other forms of body language. But the communication acquires quite another precision when language is used, when verbal communication and verbal transmission occurs. By verbal tradition I mean words, utterances, texts, writings, etc., which articulate the content of the inner tradition (both its old and its new elements). I mean not only fixed formulas and texts but also the free, flexible elements that are used in order to express the content of tradition. Basically the verbal tradition is oral. In cultures where writing has had an influential position for a long time, however, the oral language is often more or less clearly structured according to patterns of the written language; here the interaction between the written and the spoken word is a very interesting problem.

Language plays an immensely vital role for almost all efficient transmission of tradition.[4] Certainly human beings can hand over much to each other and to future generations without words, but normally language plays a key role in most kinds of transmission of tradition. With language we can fix an idea, take care of it in an effective way, and spread it through a communication which is more

---

[4] Müller writes: "Keine Tradition funktioniert nämlich ohne Sprache," *Traditionsprozess*, 15. For my part I would not go that far.

distinct and explicit than other forms of outer tradition. As a rule the different forms of outer tradition interact, but the verbal tradition is without doubt the most influential of them all. With the aid of language we can steer the course of tradition, indicate the programmatic center of it, make distinctions and specifications, revise or alter it, and so on.

(2) Behavioral tradition (practical tradition). The inner life of humans externalizes itself in different behaviors as well. A prominent, influential human being transmits consciously and unconsciously his way of appearing and acting to others. A basic mechanism is the fact that spontaneously we imitate those humans we look up to, venerate, admire, and love. The authoritative, admired human being is a message *per se*. Parents, teachers, leaders, and other "impressive" men or women become pattern-forming. We speak of the force of example and demand that persons in official position be irreproachable and set good examples. Presumably this mechanism of imitation often corresponds to the proclivity of the influential individual to externalize himself forcefully in the fellowship, come forward from obscurity and silence, assert his influence, get his own way, set the tone, or whatever we may call it. In this way the programmatic part of the behavioral tradition tends to concentrate on that which the influential individuals want to pass on.

(3) Institutional tradition. Vital inner tradition creates—at least if it is of a religious nature—engagement and fellowship. And every human community organizes itself and institutionalizes itself. The process starts immediately. A fellowship is formed and a gulf begins growing between insiders and outsiders; and furthermore, within the former role division, hierarchy and organization develop. If this did not happen, the members would be nothing but isolated individuals, only loosely connected to each other, and the group would soon dissolve. To create coherent community these mechanisms are necessary: social fellowship, order, organization, structures, establishments.[5] Long experience tells us also that such phenomena are

---

[5] See B. Holmberg, *Paul and Power: The Structure of Authority in the Primitive Church as Reflected in the Pauline Epistles* (ConBNT 11; Lund: Gleerup, 1978; Philadelphia: Fortress, 1980).

hard to destroy once they have developed, and difficult to change or abolish. This I call institutional tradition.

(4) Material tradition. It is reasonable that we also discern a fourth form of outer tradition. The inner tradition often needs to use inanimate objects as means: specific localities, special clothes, tools, or other outward equipment may be vital for the efficient function of tradition. This we may designate as material tradition.[6]

2. Commentary

In the ideal case these different aspects function in interaction. The carriers, filled by the inner tradition, effectively make use of the different parts of the outer tradition. New members are won and socialized into this multidimensional tradition. When this process is successful, the new tradition is *internalized* in the new member so that he becomes a genuine and living traditionist himself. In such cases the differentiation of aspects may appear somewhat artificial.

But the situation is not often an ideal one. The different aspects of a rich tradition do not belong together *by necessity:* they must *be kept* together by an inner engagement. And they are different even in regard to mobility and flexibility. The inner tradition may be very mobile—develop, change, be renewed—without the outward forms being able to keep pace with it. The outer forms have a rigidity and fixity which the inner tradition does not have. *Intra muros* some people may accept parts of the outer tradition but not all of it, and they may even adopt most of the outer tradition without acquiring the living inner engagement. *Extra muros* an outsider can come across single, isolated elements from this tradition: get an inanimate object in his hand without knowing how to use it, meet forms of organization that he can do nothing but wonder about, see behavior that appears meaningless to him, hear words that he cannot understand. This shows that it is meaningful in an investigation to separate the different aspects so that we can speak about them one by one when necessary (often it is not at all necessary).

---

[6] In my earlier writings (e.g., *The Origins*) I did not separate "material tradition" as a specific aspect but included it in the "institutional tradition."

I should perhaps mention two more observations of a general kind. The outward forms of tradition are—when they emerge—motivated and more or less necessary. Otherwise they would not arise so regularly. But they are also *problematic*. First, they are as a rule conventionalizing elements as such. Few people can verbalize their inward experiences in totally adequate words, least of all their deepest and most overwhelming experiences. Few people can create new words, expressions, texts. We must more or less all make use of linguistic means which already exist, when we want to verbalize our experiences and communicate them to others. Already at the first verbalization the original idea becomes domesticated and conventionalized to some extent.

The same applies to our behavior. Few people are radically creative in their behavior and actions. Already existing patterns are taken into use as models, with minor or major alterations. Even with regard to organization and institutional forms human imagination is limited; in addition we are dominated by certain general mechanisms of a sociopsychological character. Social organization and institutionalized forms are seldom radically new. A new movement must as a rule content itself with existing forms in its first phase. This fact reduces its possibility of being original. In all dimensions we see that the outer forms of tradition are intrinsically more or less domesticating and conventionalizing factors.

Second, outer tradition tends to become independent and function mechanically. These fixed forms can be in use even when there is no inward engagement behind them. And once they are well established they generally are very difficult to reform or exchange. Therefore, they usually keep their form a long time even when the inner tradition has developed and changed so as to require altered or new outward forms. The history of religion is full of pious words and texts, which many people take to their lips but only few follow in life and action; rites, habits, and customs which long ago lost their original rationale but are still practiced; institutional forms which go on in their beaten tracks in spite of the fact that they hinder rather than serve their original aims; things outdated and unfit that should have been discarded centuries ago but are still in use. In sum: inner tradition needs outer tradition, but the latter is always problematic; it must be under permanent supervision if it is to continue to be an adequate tool for the inner tradition.

3. Programmatic Tradition and De Facto Tradition

No new tradition makes all things new. Emotionally it can be felt to do so, and the mottoes can imply that it does so, but in real life a new tradition initially changes nothing but a small, illuminated circle within the existing realities.[7] If, however, the new tradition is strong and vital, it widens its area successively: ever more of the inherited realities are taken up in the light of new awareness and made the object of consideration and decision, with or without alterations.

In order to keep this in mind one must, I think, make a distinction between programmatic tradition and the de facto tradition. The former designation stands for that which is new or permeated by the new tradition, the latter for the immense older tradition which is still there without having been consciously accepted or consciously rejected.

The de facto tradition is of interest from many angles, not only as the mother-womb which has given birth to the new tradition and as the mother-breast on which it can live for a long time. An important problem is the fact that even leading representatives of the new tradition may spread much older, uncontrolled de facto tradition: they practice old values and behavior which they have not contemplated and spread them without being aware of it.

In the sources, de facto tradition is difficult to come to grips with. That which is common and self-evident is only mentioned by accident in the sources. In contrast the sources provide an effective witness about the programmatic tradition: one is occupied with this, one speaks about this. This fact is especially evident when the traditionists expressly indicate that this shall be observed and maintained as tradition: *phylassein, tērein, histanai, katechein, kratein,* etc.[8] Even a summons to take heed, listen, see and hear, and the like, is telling, as are exhortations to receive or accept.

---

[7] Cf. *Tradition* (n. 2), 22–23.
[8] Cf. O. Cullmann, *Die Tradition als exegetisches, historisches und theologisches Problem* (Zürich: Zwingli, 1954), 12–16; *Memory* (n. 2), 288–91, and *Origins,* sect. 5 (above).

II. CHRISTIANITY'S JEWISH MOTHER-TRADITION

In its first formative period, early Christianity was influenced from many quarters. It would, however, be a serious historical mistake to put these influences on the same level. One of them must be placed in a class by itself and called the mother-tradition of Christianity. Jesus, the Twelve, and almost all leaders in the first decades of early Christianity were Jews by birth and upbringing, being socialized in the Jewish tradition. Jesus confined himself almost exclusively to the Jewish population of Palestine, and the early Christian mission was primarily directed to Jews or proselytes—and other people who were already attracted by Judaism. Christianity was born within Judaism. Neither Jesus nor the church in its first decades ever wanted to be anything else than Israel: they looked upon themselves as the *true* Israel. Their message presented news from Israel's God: what he now wanted to do and what he now had to say to his people—in a new time. In one way we could say that the original Christian message can be regarded as a concentration and radicalization of the ancient belief within the covenant between Israel and its God.

Early Christianity initially felt at home in Judaism and from it inherited considerable inhibitions and reservations concerning other cults and everything connected with them: paganism, heathenism! Therefore we have every reason to call ancient Judaism early Christianity's mother-tradition. This must not prevent a full consideration of the fact that the Jews were "Hellenized" to a considerable degree at this time, even the Jews in Palestine. Nor must it prevent us from seeing the influences from different Hellenistic traditions that had their impact nonetheless upon Christian communities during the decades—and centuries—which followed.

Let us now apply our model to ancient Judaism, let us say from 200 B.C. to A.D. 200.

1. Inner Tradition

The Jews in Palestine at the beginning of our Christian era constituted a relatively pluralistic society. Yet, it does not seem farfetched to speak of "Judaism" at that time—they themselves used the term *ioudaïsmos*[9]—and to take the pious, religiously active Jews as the most representative Jews, at least when we are looking for the mother-tradition of Christianity. To these Jews, Jewish identity and inherited tradition in its totality was a programmatic concern, the Torah tradition in all its aspects.

This Jewish tradition was immensely rich and multifarious. Yet, it had a vital inner life: the Torah-centric relation to "the only true God" with its different elements: faith, love, obedience, loyalty in emotions and thought, in word and action, toward God; and a corresponding attitude toward fellow human beings. To the pious representatives of the Torah tradition this was a conscious program. They wanted to stand in covenant with God, and tradition showed what this covenant meant in its different aspects. As to Israel as a people, the temple, the syna-gogues, the schools, and other institutions were devoted to God and revealed his gifts and his demands.[10] As to the individual pious man, the center of the covenant and the Torah tradition is made clear to him, when twice a day he personally actualizes the covenant by reciting the Shema. First he takes "the yoke of the reign of heaven" upon himself by affirming God's sovereign position as the only true God with the words: "The Lord our God, the Lord is one Lord." Then he takes upon himself "the yoke of the commandments," all of them in condensed form, by accepting the claim that he shall love the Lord his God with his whole heart, his whole soul, and all his resources. Before Him who is One, God's people and every member of it shall be one. Here, as in many other ways, we see the program that everything shall be put under the grace and will of God and that the individual as well as the people shall accept all of it. Thus, a strong tendency toward unity is characteristic for the leading representatives of the Torah tradition.[11]

Of course we must consider the de facto pluralism in Israel when trying to make a careful detailed description of the situation. How much of the rich heritage had at this time been consciously taken into the spotlight, invented, and regulated? How many of the

---

[9] E.g., 2 Macc 2:21; 8:1; 14:38. Cf. Gal 1:13–14. Note that the term is used solely in the singular; "Judaisms" is a modern manner of speaking.

[10] Cf. *Memory,* 71–78. See also Riesner, *Jesus als Lehrer* (n. 1), 97–245.

[11] [For literature on the role of the Shema in early Judaism and early Christianity, see now the author's collection of essays *The Shema in the New Testament: Deut 6:4–5 in Significant Passages* (Lund: Novapress, 1996).]

Jews did in fact accept this program wholeheartedly and in all its breadth? Where shall we put the tepid Jews? Uneducated Jews? People in isolated areas? And so forth. But these are common problems irrespective of what model we choose.

2. Outer Tradition

(1) Verbal tradition. In ancient Jewish tradition language plays an accentuated role; seeing and visions are not so much in the forefront as are words, speaking, and hearing. The Torah tradition was passed on with the aid of a rich treasure of authoritative terms, expressions, formulas, motifs, texts, and writings, preserved in an oral and written tradition with both fixed and flexible elements: Torah as words. (I do not take "Torah" in the narrow sense of "law" but in its wider sense, "teaching": all that was classified as God's authoritative teaching to his people, directly or indirectly.[12] And I repeat once more that this word-tradition had a large *flexible* sector.[13])

---

[12] Even in *Memory* I did not take the word "Torah" in the narrow meaning "law," nor "oral Torah" in the narrow meaning "the halakic rules." This seems to have escaped the notice of J. Neusner, in spite of the fact that it is stated and explained rather clearly in the first chapter of *Memory,* 19–32; it is even printed in italics: *"In this investigation we shall use the term Torah, without qualification, as a collective designation for the Jews' sacred authoritative tradition (doctrine) in its entirety"* (21). I also tried to clear away any misunderstanding about this (*Tradition,* 7). Torah does not contain texts alone, nor are all texts legal rules. Again, my designation "verbal tradition" not only covers texts but all other authoritative teaching expressed in words as well, even flexible words; "verbal" here means "articulated" (see *Tradition,* 7). In addition, when I say that the written Torah must always have had oral Torah at its side, I do not mean that Moses received the rabbinic halakic rules on Sinai but simply that no lawmaker can express *everything* in his brief written rules; from the very beginning the text needs oral complements, exposition, and additional teaching. I regret that Neusner, who has clarified important aspects of rabbinic halakic tradition so brilliantly (cf. below n. 70), has presented my position as if I was an old Jewish fundamentalist, believing that the halakic rules of the tannaitic and amoraic rabbis were received by Moses on Sinai in their present form; see, e.g., Neusner, *The Rabbinic Traditions about the Pharisees before 70* (3 vols; Leiden: Brill, 1971), vol. 3, 146–48; 163–77; and "The Rabbinic Traditions about the Pharisees before 70 A.D.: The Problem of Oral Tradition," *Kairos* 14 (1972): 57–70.

[13] See above n. 12 and below nn. 44 and 57.

(2) Behavioral tradition. "The life in the Torah" (*hē ennomos biōsis,* Sir prol. 14) was eminently an inherited, characteristic way of life, conscious patterns for the way in which the people and different groups and individuals should live: rites, customs, ethos, halakah. Here we meet Torah as practice.[14]

(3) Institutional tradition. The faithful Jews also maintained a rich inheritance of institutions and establishments, social structures, hierarchy, official divisions of role, and more of the same. Even this was accepted as ordered by God; this was Torah as institution.

(4) Material tradition. The Torah tradition finally included sacred localities, clothes, tools, and other outward things: the temple buildings, synagogue rooms, scrolls, phylacteries, tassels on cloaks, etc., things of importance for life in the Torah. If the expression can be allowed, I would like to call it Torah as "things."

III. THE EARLY CHRISTIAN TRADITION

We will now see how our model separates different aspects within the early Christian tradition. Let me start with a brief survey.

1. Survey: Inner and Outer Tradition

Inner tradition. The heart of early Christianity was a Jesus Christ–centered relation to God: faith, love, obedience, loyalty, etc., and a corresponding attitude toward fellow human beings. Paul's designation was "life in Christ."

Outer tradition. (1) Verbal tradition. The programmatic speaking of early Christianity has a center: Jesus Christ, interpreted as the decisive, final Savior and Lord. One speaks about him, preaches about him, teaches about him, quotes sayings from him, and tells narratives about him. Texts arise, some quite fixed, some more or less flexible. Gradually, smaller or larger written records are made, and letters are written about his mysteries. As time goes on more comprehensive writings are composed. In a living interaction we

---

[14] For an illustration, see *Memory* (n. 2), 181–89.

meet here fixed and flexible elements with all kinds of intermediate forms: the Christ tradition as words.

(2) Behavioral tradition. Early Christianity, inheriting Jewish behavioral tradition and at its core dominated by the practice and teaching of Jesus, develops a characteristic way of life. It is rich and variegated, but it is very revealing that the program for the adherents of Jesus is called "the life in Christ," "following Jesus," or "imitation of Christ." Here we meet the Christ tradition as practice.[15]

(3) Institutional tradition. Jesus attracts a central group of adherents, binds them to his person and becomes their exclusive leader and inspirer. A delimited group is formed around him and an elementary organization starts developing. After the departure of its sole master this group must be reconstructed and reorganized. This hastens the process of institutionalization; division of roles, hierarchy, and organization develop. The Christ tradition assumes institutional forms.

(4) Material tradition. So far as outward things are concerned, the Jesus movement and the young church do not need any specifically new things at the beginning. They take what they need from their mother-tradition. Not until later does the specifically Christian material tradition become interesting.

2. Inner Tradition

Looking backward historically, we see that Jesus initiates a new tradition in the bosom of the Jewish mother-tradition. It is not difficult to understand that this historical volcanic eruption begins as an inner tradition; a strong conviction of faith and a firm consciousness of vocation makes Jesus turn to the community ("to appear publicly before Israel") in order to influence his people with words and deeds. Within the mother-tradition ("the covenant") he concentrates on the basic statements about God and his mighty deeds and proclaims to his people that God's power will soon be manifested in a new way.

---

[15] Note the expression *ennomos Christou* in 1 Cor 9:21; cf. *hē ennomos biōsis* in the Sirach prologue. Cf. further E. Larsson, *Christus als Vorbild: Eine Untersuchung zu den paulinischen Tauf- und Eikontexten* (ASNU 23; Lund: Gleerup, Copenhagen: Munksgaard, 1962), and E. Cothenet, 'Imitation du Christ,' *Dictionnaire de spiritualité*, fasc. 48–49 (1970), 1536–82.

It will soon be seen what it means that God is God: the Lord is One and only One is the Lord. In this perspective he calls his people to repentance and inculcates the other side of the matter: God's people shall love God with their whole heart and their whole soul and all their resources.[16]

The demand that the community and the individual shall be "perfect" in their inner life (their "heart") and thus undivided, whole, and without blemish or defect before God was a basic ideal in the mother-tradition, but Jesus accentuated it with a new radicalism. We then notice that the leaders in the young church share this engagement with its total demands. Certainly Luke's notice in Acts 4:32 paints a very idealized picture of the Christian mother-community in Jerusalem, but the words are telling: "the whole company of those who believed were of one heart and one soul, and no one said that any of the things which he possessed was his own, but they had everything in common."[17] Many passages in the New Testament stress the demands for unity and consistency: one shall be a Christ-centered worshiper of God in everything. And the communities shall be united and unanimous in spite of a legitimate variety, inspired by one and the same Spirit, have one mind, "think the same," and so forth.[18]

If one is aware of the complexity of the problems and the potential complications, it is thus possible to regard early Christianity as a new tradition with an eruptive center of inner tradition which expresses itself in words and behavior, forms a new fellowship with incipient institutionalization very early, and in the long run also has its consequences as to outward things.

Of course, the most important question concerns the character and content of the inner tradition, but I cannot stop to discuss this matter now.[19]

---

[16] See, e.g., my book *The Ethos of the Bible* (Philadelphia: Fortress, 1981; London: Darton, Longman & Todd, 1982).

[17] See my article "Einige Bemerkungen zu Apg 4,32," *Studia Theologica* 24 (1970): 142–49, reprinted in *The Shema in the New Testament* (n. 11), 239–46.

[18] See, e.g., Acts 2:44–47; 4:32; Rom 12:3–13; 15:5–6; 1 Cor 1:10–13; 12:4–31; Eph 4:1–16; Phil 1:27; 2:1–4; 3:15–16; Col 3:14–15—not to speak of ethical texts like Matt 5:17–48. See further my book *The Ethos of the Bible* (n. 16).

[19] [I have tried to do so in other connections; see the literature mentioned in the preface to this book.]

3. Outer Tradition

As we shall deal at length with the gospel tradition I shall comment on the verbal tradition last, despite the fact that doing so puts the four aspects of outer tradition in reverse order.

A. Material tradition

The theme "early Christianity and material tradition" is a fascinating subject, still not very well clarified: What role did the temple, the synagogues, Torah scrolls, phylacteries, and the like play for Jesus and early Christianity; how did the development go, and how did early Christianity's own material tradition evolve? We must of course consider the various components separately and also distinguish between different persons, groups, geographic areas, and phases in the development of early Christianity. The attitudes varied. Those who had markedly spiritualized views and regarded Christianity as a "worship in spirit and truth" and those who remained faithful attendees at the temple and synagogue and continued to respect phylacteries, etc., cannot all be treated alike. Pauline and Johannine areas were not totally similar, nor do the oldest of the Pauline Letters reflect the same situation as the Pastoral Letters.

Telling is the strong difference between the Christians' attitude to the religious material tradition among the Jews and their attitude to things connected with pagan cults and pagan sacred practices.

In general I think we can say that the attitude to Jewish material tradition is a combination of familiarity, freedom, and incipient liberation. The crux of the matter is the fact that the inner tradition generated great freedom toward all outward things, even the most religious ones. One could do equally well with them or without them. Certainly the Christian Jews mourned when the temple fell, but their own divine service was not interrupted. Certainly it was extremely distressing for them to leave the synagogue fellowship when doing so became necessary, but their own worship could continue just the same; the choice of some other place was no matter of principle. How the Christian Jews stopped using phylacteries, tassels, and the like we do not even know. The development was obviously so undramatic that no source has noted it.

Of course, development toward a specifically Christian material tradition started quite early. Certain things gradually became sacred; localities with certain furnishings, clothes, eucharistic vessels, etc. But we do not see much of this in the New Testament.

Of special interest is the question of the attitude to holy books, both as holy writ and as sacred objects. Jesus and the leading figures in early Christianity certainly ascribed to the opinion that the ancient holy scriptures should be treated with veneration, even as scrolls. Nothing indicates, however, that the writings and books produced by early Christianity itself were immediately regarded as holy scriptures, even less as sacred objects. The book of Revelation is a possible exception (see 1:1–3; 22:18–19). If notebooks were used, they were simply private aids, not holy scriptures. They are not even mentioned in the New Testament. The only books of which we catch a glimpse are the ancient holy scriptures. The written gospels—presumably in codex form—were not initially regarded as holy scriptures or sacred books. This did not come until later.

I shall not linger on this. However, I will stress once more that this aspect—material tradition—is also important for a realistic historical picture of the gospel tradition during the first century.

B. Institutional tradition

Jesus and early Christianity existed in a world which was well institutionalized: politically, economically, socially, religiously, from the greatest structures of the Roman Empire down to the individual families, Jewish and non-Jewish alike. Jesus and the Christians were dependent upon this and accepted very much of it.[20] To the extent that these different institutions had any importance for early Christianity's programmatic tradition, we must take them into consideration. We must study the spectrum of radical to conservative attitudes to these different institutions, in principle and in practice, in order to gain an adequate picture of the early Christian tradition.

---

[20] From a theological point of view one thing is especially interesting in this connection: the fact that Jesus and his followers consciously refrained from making *political* responsibility their own cause. They presupposed that the different political rulers had a mission from God, which Jesus did not want to take from them: God's "secular realm" (Luther)!

More important for our investigation of the gospel tradition, however, is the process of institutionalization within early Christianity itself. Two things are especially interesting:

(1) Jesus not only attracts throngs of people who listen to him accidentally or for some short period, and sympathizers at various places in Palestine. He gathers around himself a number of persons who become his "primary group": they "are with" him *(einai meta)*, they "follow" *(akolouthein)* him, they are his "disciples" *(mathētai)*, they are his "brother and sister and mother."[21] This information in our sources is extremely important from a phenomenological point of view. We recognize the pattern: the strong and exclusive gathering around Jesus creates an incipient gulf between insiders and outsiders, a gulf which becomes even more pronounced when the Jesus movement is reconstructed after Easter.

(2) Within this primary group emerges an embryonic organization: a certain ranking becomes natural, a certain distribution of roles, etc. Twelve disciples have a special position as a kind of symbolic collegium around the Master; three of them constitute an inner circle and one of these is the *primus.* It seems to me very likely that Jesus himself took the initiative to organize his closest adherents in this elementary fashion. Even if he did not, it is easy to explain that this organization originated very soon in the most permanent fellowship around him; that is the way fellowship generally behaves!

If we consider this fact—institutional tradition in early Christianity—we can be rather sure about one thing. The followers of Jesus—before and after his departure—did not think that the truth about their master was to be found among the outsiders. Of course, rumors were spread about Jesus. Even if our sources did not say a word to that effect, we should be rather sure that rumors went out *(diaphēmizein)* and that many people heard about the fame of Jesus

---

[21] Examples: "to be with" *(einai meta)*, Mark 3:14; 5:18; 14:67; Matt 26:69, 71; Luke 22:59; *(einai syn)*, Luke 8:38; 22:56; "to follow" *(akolouthein)*, Mark 1:18; 2:14; 8:34; 10:21, 28; Matt 4:20, 22; 8:19, 22; 9:9; 10:38; 16:24; 19:21, 27, 28; Luke 5:11, 27, 28; 9:23, 57, 59, 61; 18:22, 28; John 1:43; 8:12; 12:26; 21:19, 22; "to walk after" *(erchesthai opisō)*, Mark 8:34; Matt 10:38; 16:24; Luke 9:23; 14:27; cf. also the command "follow" *(deute opisō)*, Mark 1:17; Matt 4:19; "my brother, sister, and mother," Mark 3:31–35; Matt 12:46–50; Luke 8:19–21.

(hē akoē Iēsou).[22] But our knowledge about how institutionalization progresses teaches us that an engaged and structured religious community does not think much of outsider rumors and talk. What has authority is that which is cultivated *intra muros:* here the true insights are to be found. And here, inside the walls, all do not enjoy the same authority. Some have a reputation of being especially well informed, and a preference for those in the know is general in every fellowship.[23] Simple phenomenological insights tell us that those in the best position to spread recollections and traditions about Jesus within early Christianity were those who had the reputation of being well informed, especially those who could say that they had seen with their own eyes and heard with their own ears. (Curiously, although the synoptic tradition cries out for actual originators, numerous leading New Testament scholars these days show very little inclination to credit the Twelve or anyone else with first-hand knowledge of Jesus.)[24]

C. Behavioral tradition

I very much doubt whether any nation in the world can compete with the Jewish people in detailed, sophisticated awareness of their own way of life. The development in that direction had reached very far even in New Testament times. A strong political threat from different forces of occupation and a powerful spiritual and cultural threat from the flourishing Hellenistic culture had made the Jews observant and sensitive and evoked a remarkable zeal to defend Jewish identity and tradition—*ho ioudaïsmos*—in all its

---

[22] Cf., e.g., Mark 1:45; Matt 9:31; 28:15 *(diaphēmizein);* Mark 1:28; Matt 4:24; 14:1 *(akoē)*.

[23] Some revealing New Testament texts: John 15:26–27; 19:35; 21:24; Luke 1:1–4; 24:44–49; Acts 1:1–3, 8, 21–26; 2:32; 4:19–20; 5:15–16; 29–32, etc.; 1 Cor 15:5–8, 11; 2 Cor 11:5; 12:11; Gal 1:18–20; 2:1–10; etc.

[24] In his article "*Episkopē* and *episkopos:* the New Testament Evidence," *Theological Studies* 41 (1980): 322–38, R. E. Brown concludes concerning the Twelve: "The image of them as carrying on missionary endeavors all over the world has no support in the NT or in other reliable historical sources. The archeological and later documentary evidence that Peter died at Rome is credible, but the rest of the Twelve could have died in Jerusalem so far as we have trustworthy information," 325. I think it is very proper indeed to ask what this highly reputed collegium actually *did* during its years in Jerusalem.

aspects, and not least the Jews' characteristic way of life with its many rules for religion and morality: rites, customs, ethos, halakah.

Certainly the degree of awareness, enlightenment, and actual observance varied greatly within pluralistic Judaism: from individual to individual, group to group, stratum to stratum, area to area. From this point of view the disciples of Jesus presumably had rather different backgrounds. The diversity was even greater later on when the church included people from many different parts of the Roman empire and not only Jews.

For a study of the gospel tradition, an investigation of Jesus' and early Christianity's relations to the Jewish behavioral tradition is extremely important, especially in the light of Jesus' admonition to put one's confession and insights into practice: to "do" the word.[25] Very roughly speaking, the pattern of Jesus' own attitude to the behavioral aspect of the Jewish mother-tradition is that he shows very little interest in halakic minutiae but a very strong interest in the central ethos of the mother-tradition, which may be summarized in formulas such as "the great and first commandment" (Matt 22:38), "the weightiest matters of the law" (Matt 23:23), or in some other way. His own "new teaching" is a radicalization of the central core within the verbal Torah.[26]

The fact that the ethical teaching of Jesus was strongly centered around the basic norms indicates that he focused the interest of his adherents upon these. This also means—and it is important to observe this—that he even made their practical *imitation* of him rather specific. When in love, admiration, and veneration they emulated their master, it was natural to pay the greatest attention to that which was a central concern for the Master himself and imitate him in such matters, not in various outward details. Thus the imitation of Jesus assumed a profile different from the imitation of rabbis with different specializations even though the same sociopsychological mechanisms were at work in both cases.[27]

---

[25] I am thinking of all texts where the motif is present, not only of passages containing the verb *poiein*.

[26] See, e.g., my book *Ethos* (n. 16), 33–62, 124–26, and cf. H. Braun, *Spätjüdisch-häretischer und frühchristlicher Radikalismus* (BHT 24; 2 vols; Tübingen: Mohr [Siebeck], 1957).

[27] This is my answer to M. Hengel, *Nachfolge und Charisma: Eine exegetisch-religionsgeschichtliche Studie zu Mt 8,21f. und Jesu Ruf in die*

This we see very clearly in Paul. When he suggests Christ as a model, he never mentions concrete details in Jesus' conduct but always the central principle in his attitude: his self-sacrificing love demonstrated in action. We can certainly say that all of Paul's direct references to Jesus as an ethical model are concrete examples of *agapē*. We also see that Paul sometimes puts forward himself and even other prominent representatives of Jesus' ethos as secondary models for imitation. It should be noted that he aims at the true reception of the message from and about Jesus Christ, thus as words and as a practical life accordingly.[28]

So much for the *general* (primarily ethical) behavioral tradition. But some *specific* parts of early Christianity's behavioral tradition also deserve attention if we want to put the gospel tradition in a realistic historical framework: (1) rites in the context of worship, (2) practices in teaching and other specific forms of verbal transmission, (3) therapeutic activity.

(1) It goes without saying that the forms of early Christian worship were borrowed from Jewish practice: liturgical praying, recitation and singing, sacred meals, and so on. We can call this the "liturgical tradition of behavior."

(2) Most interesting for the study of the gospel tradition is of course the specific behavior of verbal communication and transmission, the forms for reading, teaching, exhortation, discussions, and so forth, both the genuine Jewish models with their different degrees of Hellenization and the subsequent side-influences from different traditions in the early Christian milieus. This I shall discuss at length shortly.

(3) A third area requiring special attention concerns therapeutic practices in early Christianity: healings and exorcisms, carried out in accordance with the example and, perhaps, instructions of Jesus. This seems to have taken different forms: a more charismatic one,

---

Nachfolge (BZNW 34; Berlin: Töpelmann, 1968), 46–79; ET *The Charismatic Leader and His Followers* (trans. J. C. G. Greig; Edinburgh: T&T Clark, 1981). He paints a sharp contrast between Jesus and the rabbis. In my opinion Hengel overlooks here the general sociopsychological mechanisms which operate in both contexts, in spite of all differences.

[28] On the imitation motif among the rabbis, see *Memory* (n. 2), 181–89; on the motif in the Pauline material, see 292–94 and *Ethos* (n. 16), 72–76, 89–90, 124–26.

handled by individuals with a specific gift of healing (*charisma iamatōn;* cf. 1 Cor 12:9), and one of a more institutionalized character, handled by specific persons in office (cf. Mark 6:7–13; James 5:14–15), with possible combinations and intermediate forms. This aspect of the behavioral tradition is of interest because it was programmatic for Jesus and early Christianity: to the central task belonged not only preaching and teaching but also healing and exorcism.[29] Therefore we must investigate this part of the behavioral tradition and its relation to the gospel tradition.[30] Which older models did Jesus himself link up with, totally or in part? To what extent was his own practice an object of imitation? To what extent did he give direct instructions? What role did concrete traditions about Jesus' teaching and therapeutic practice—the gospel tradition—play for early Christianity's practice in this respect? And can we reckon with the possibility that therapeutic practices in the church after Easter have influenced the gospel tradition?

D. Verbal tradition

In order to emphasize the need for concreteness in our historical reconstruction and interpretation of the transmission of the gospel tradition, I have tried in the foregoing pages to draw the reader's attention to pertinent mechanisms in early Christian tradition which must be taken into consideration when working with the concrete Jesus tradition. We are now prepared to enter the central area of our subject, early Christianity's verbal tradition. I will group my observations and reflections under ten headings.

a. The information in the Lukan prologue

Let me start with some general comments on the prologue to Luke-Acts (Luke 1:1–4). This is the most important item of information which is preserved from the first Christian centuries about the prehistory of the Gospels. The fragments of information in Papias,

---

[29] See, e.g., Mark 1:39; Matt 4:23; 9:35; Luke 4:16–24, 31–37, 40–41, and Mark 3:13–15; Matt 10:1–8; Luke 9:1–2; Acts 3:6; 4:29–30; 5:12–16.

[30] For literature on the miracles of Jesus, see my book *The Mighty Acts of Jesus according to Matthew* (Scripta minora 1978–1979, 9; Lund: Gleerup, 1979). On healing as a vital part of Jesus' activity in Israel, see pp. 20–51.

Irenaeus, Clement, the prologues, etc.,[31] certainly deserve all the
interest they have received. But these notices are not as old as the
Lukan prologue and they seem to give a somewhat anachronistic
picture of the origin of the Gospels. They hardly reveal any awareness of two important facts: that the Gospels build upon a common
oral tradition and that there must also be some kind of literary connection between them, at least between the Synoptics. In this material from the ancient church we get the picture of an individual
teacher who had preached and taught with great authority and then
wrote down his material himself (Matthew, John) or had some fol-
lower commit his teaching to writing (Mark, Luke). I do not think
these items of information are freely made up, but they seem to give
us a somewhat anachronistic picture.

Let me quote the ancient prologue to Luke's two-volume work
(Luke 1:1–4):

> Since many writers have undertaken to compile an orderly account
> of the events that have come to fulfillment among us, just as the
> original eyewitnesses and ministers of the word passed them on to
> us, I too have decided, after tracing everything carefully from the
> beginning, to put them systematically in writing for you, Theophilus,
> so that Your Excellency may realize what assurance you have for the
> instruction you have received.[32]

Seven points should be observed in this brief text.

(1) "Luke" wants to present an orderly account *(diēgēsis)* of the
Jesus events, but he indicates that this attempt is innovative. Like a
number of predecessors, he has felt the need and made the attempt to
put together the material about Jesus into an organized, synthetic presentation, but the material did not have this form from the beginning.

(2) Luke classifies his material as tradition and indicates that it
is insider tradition, which is there *intra muros ecclesiae*. It is all about

---

[31] The most important material from the fathers is conveniently
brought together in K. Aland, *Synopsis quattuor evangeliorum* (Stuttgart:
Württembergische Bibelanstalt, 1964), 531–48. See also W. Rordorf, A.
Schneider, *Die Entwicklung des Traditionsbegriffs in der Alten Kirche*
(Traditio christiana 5; Bern and Frankfurt a.M.: Peter Lang, 1983).

[32] Fitzmyer's translation. On the exegetical problems in Luke 1:1–4,
see J. A. Fitzmyer, *The Gospel according to Luke I–IX* (AB 28; New York:

"events that have come to fulfillment among us"; the information has "been passed on to us" *(paredōsan hēmin)*. This means that the material has been preserved and exists within the church.

(3) Luke also mentions the originators of the material. The traditions stem from "the original eyewitnesses *(autoptai)* and ministers of the word." In the Lukan usage this means the closest followers and disciples of Jesus, first of all the Twelve but hardly exclusively.

(4) The originators are called not only "eyewitnesses" but also "ministers of the word" *(hypēretai tou logou)*. Thus, they have not only quoted and reported what they had heard and seen but have also been active as ministers of the word as well, which must mean that they have preached, taught, expounded the scriptures, and so on. In Acts 6:4 their main activity is called "ministry of the Word" *(diakonia tou logou)*.

(5) Luke knows about many earlier attempts to compile an orderly account of the Jesus event. "Many" *(polloi)* is certainly a conventional exaggeration, but Luke would hardly use this phrase if he was just thinking of one or two specific predecessors.

(6) For his own part Luke had a special purpose when he wrote his gospel. It is a matter of dispute whether his words about his own carefulness imply criticism of his predecessors. If so, he expresses himself so discreetly that the reader who is not already suspicious does not notice it. One thing, however, Luke expresses clearly. He has a special purpose which his predecessors obviously did not have: his ambition is to write history (cf. also 1:5; 2:1–2; 3:1–2). This aim makes him combine two subjects which usually were kept apart: on the one hand the teaching, work, and fate of Jesus, and on the other hand the fate of the Christian message during the first decades of the church.[33] Luke's way of dedicating his work to the illustrious Theophilus gives us reason for believing that his opus is not written for the communities but for cultivated individuals within the church and presumably also outside it: for the public market.[34] This confers on the Gospel of Luke a *specific* nature which must be kept in mind

---

Doubleday, 1981), 287–302, and H. Schürmann, *Das Lukasevangelium* (HTKNT 3:1; Freiburg, Basel, Wien: Herder, 1969), 1–17.

[33] Cf. I. H. Marshall, "Luke and his 'Gospel'," *The Gospel and the Gospels* (ed. P. Stuhlmacher; Grand Rapids: Eerdmans, 1991), 273–92.

[34] Cf. M. Dibelius, *Aufsätze zur Apostelgeschichte* (FRLANT 60; 5th ed.; Göttingen: Vandenhoeck & Ruprecht, 1968), 79 and 118.

both in the discussion about Luke's way of handling the oral tradition and in the analysis of the relations between the three Synoptic Gospels.[35]

(7) Luke reveals here—as he does in the main text of his work as well—that he has a general respect for reliable tradition and faithful traditionists. I do not think it is correct to interpret this respect as nothing but a secondary feature, due to point in time, the individuality of the author, or his special purpose. It seems to be a typical insider evaluation: respect for one's own group's tradition and a preference for those in the know.

b. Oral and written transmission

Language is a vocal means of communication; it is spoken, it sounds, it is heard. As we are presently dealing with antiquity—thus not the era of the printed word or of silent reading—it is important to keep in mind that even the *written* word is a vocal word. It is very misleading if, in our discussions about conditions in antiquity, we put oral and written delivery side by side on the same level as two entirely comparable entities and proclaim that the one is made for the eye, the other for the ear.[36] In antiquity, words were written down in order to be read out. Even the written word was formulated for the ear. One read aloud when reading for oneself or asked a slave or a friend to read aloud. (Public reading was also common.) There is much evidence for this in the sources, both from the Greco-Roman and from the Jewish worlds. The author *speaks,* and the reader speaks as well; the reader *hears* what the text *says,* even when reading alone, and so on.[37] Even the copyists used to read vocally when they copied.

This also means that it is misleading to say that the written word is *visual.* Before the eye stands nothing but marks: letters, lines,

---

[35] Cf. W. C. van Unnik, "Remarks on the Purpose of Luke's Historical Writing (Luke 1:1–4)," *Sparsa collecta* (NovTSup 29–31; 3 vols.; Leiden: Brill, 1973), 1:6–15.

[36] Thus W. H. Kelber, *The Oral and the Written Gospel: The Hermeneutics of Speaking and Writing in the Synoptic Tradition, Mark, Paul, and Q* (Philadelphia: Fortress, 1983), passim.

[37] See above all J. Balogh, "Voces paginarum," *Philologus* 82 (1926–27): 84–109, 202–40, and further G. L. Hendrickson, "Ancient

columns. The illiterate can see no more than this visual image. To be able to read is to be able to change letters and lines into functioning language: otherwise one cannot understand the text. This was especially obvious in the youth of the art of writing, during the millennia when one read aloud. The writing down means that the spoken word is frozen in order to be thawed and revived as language, as a spoken word. Therefore, oral devices are very self-evident even in written texts: rhythm, meter, euphony, paronomasia, alliteration, and the like. It is a great mistake to believe that the written word was something totally different from the spoken word in antiquity. This applies both to the Greco-Roman and to the Near Eastern cultures.

During recent generations some very interesting research has been devoted to orality in societies where writing has not yet influenced language. Attempts have been made, not least by English and American scholars, to clarify how the purely spoken word functions and how a purely oral tradition is handed on.[38] It is very clear that writing influences the thinking and speaking in the direction of discursiveness and linearity; it may even influence the experience itself. But pure orality can be found only in a few societies. In "civilized" societies untouched orality is dead almost everywhere. In societies where writings have been in use for a long time it is very hard to find source material that is completely uninfluenced by writing. On the other hand, it is of course important to remember that even in our own "developed" societies the oral language has preserved certain parts of its distinctiveness and has succeeded in doing so in the face of the written language in a surprisingly tenacious way.

In his very interesting book *The Oral and the Written Gospel* (1983), Werner Kelber has made a broad attempt to interpret the early Christian process of tradition with the help of the modern folk-

---

Reading," *The Classical Journal* 25 (1929–30): 182–96, and E. S. McCartney, "Notes on Reading and Praying Audibly," *Classical Philology* 43 (1948): 184–87. On the conditions in the ancient Near East, see O. Roller, *Das Formular der paulinischen Briefe: Ein Beitrag zur Lehre vom antiken Briefe* (BWANT 58; Stuttgart: Kohlhammer, 1933), 220–23; rabbinic material in S. Krauss, *Talmudische Archäologie* (*Schriften*, ed. by Ges. zur Förd. der Wiss. des Judent.; 3 vols.; Leipzig: Fock, 1912), 3:227–29. See also *Memory*, 163–68, and cf. n. 82 below.

[38] For literature, see Kelber, *The Oral and the Written Gospel*, 227–39.

lorist model of orality. His point of departure is that there is a decisive and consistent difference of principle between orality (oral
delivery, always flexible) and textuality (written delivery). In his view
proper texts are to be found solely within written tradition. From
here they may enter the realm of oral tradition as memorized texts,
but that causes no change: now they are borrowed, and if they have a
fixed wording they are a foreign body in the oral context. Orality is
always characterized by flexibility: the speaker adapts his words to
his listeners; in one way these influence his speaking so strongly that
sender, message, and receivers form a synthetic unity: "the oral synthesis."[39] In orality the narrator takes his raw material from an inherited stock-in-trade of words, formulas, motifs, themes, plots,
devices, etc., but he never formulates his presentation of the tradition in exactly the same way twice. Every delivery (performance) is a
new variation; the model is "composition in transmission."[40] Now
Kelber tries to demonstrate that the Jesus tradition started as orality
and went through its most decisive alteration when the written word
could take full control, i.e., when the oral gospel tradition had become
written gospels. The first written gospel—Mark—was a revolutionary
phenomenon, a radical shift of medium: orality had become
textuality, flexibility had become a fixed entity, the audible word had
become a visible word, the living speech had become a book.

There are many good observations and stimulating points of
view in Kelber's book, and some of them could be illustrated with
material from the theological discussions in the ancient church and
at the Reformation about "the living voice of the gospel" *(viva vox
evangelii)*. Yet Kelber's approach seems to me to be basically inadequate.

The society where Jesus appeared—even the small towns in the
Galilean countryside—was no preliterary society. Nothing indicates
that the formative milieu of Jesus was not at all or only to a small degree influenced by the written word. It seems quite clear that the
holy scriptures were held in high regard in the family and synagogue
community in which Jesus grew up, and that influences from these
writings strongly affected thinking and speaking in this milieu as
well as Jesus himself. Nor is there any doubt that Jesus had obtained

---

[39] Ibid., 19, 40 (n. 179), 147, 168–77.
[40] Ibid., 30 and passim.

a considerable education in reading the holy scriptures—including memorizing of the texts—and was strongly influenced by this extensive text material. All the scriptural words, formulas, motifs, and patterns as well as allusions and quotations that we meet in the recorded sayings of Jesus cannot possibly be secondary altogether.

The verbal Jesus tradition was at no stage pure "orality" in the meaning theorists of orality give the term. Already in the mind of Jesus the incipient parts of the gospel tradition were influenced by an older tradition which was partly oral, partly written, and the gospel tradition retained in many ways this contact the whole time until the final redaction of the Synoptic Gospels, and afterwards as well.

c. The interaction between written and oral tradition

Occasionally, in certain places in his book, Kelber shows awareness of many complications,[41] but his main reasoning is always based on a view which makes a very clear contrast between the spoken and the written word: "Contemporary theorists of orality appear virtually unanimous in emphasizing the linguistic integrity of the difference between spoken versus written words."[42] When in an oral society one version of the ongoing oral narrating is committed to writing, a radical shift of media occurs, and this shift has far-reaching consequences. It seems to me, however, that this model cannot give us much help in trying to understand the relation between oral and written Torah tradition and gospel tradition in antiquity. The complicated situation can be illustrated with an example.[43] Let us imagine how a text from the written tradition, e.g., from the book of Isaiah, could function in a synagogue in Galilee in the New Testament period. The inherited message from Isaiah appeared in many different forms:

(1) It appeared in the scroll in the form of letters, lines, and columns as *ketāb*, "the writing," before the eyes, in other words as an orthographic tradition in Hebrew;

---

[41] Ibid., e.g., 17, 23, 29–30, 73–74, 93.

[42] Ibid., 14. Kelber's book contains numerous untenable generalizations of the differences between the oral and the written word.

[43] Cf. *Memory* (n. 2), 67–70 and 33–42; Riesner, *Jesus als Lehrer* (n. 1), 137–51.

(2) It was read aloud in an inherited audible wording, as *miqrā'*, "the reading," a traditional, vocal reading in the old original language;

(3) It was also mediated in a translated form, transposed to the living language of the people (Aramaic) as targum, a tradition of translation. This could be of different kinds but the most common choice was a middle way between a too literal and a too free translation. In order to make the ancient text comprehensible, the targumist adapted it (a) to the new language, (b) to a new situation (to some extent);

(4) If the reading and the targum was followed by a didactic speech, *midrāsh, derāshāh,* the content of the text could be clarified in more detail in a fourth form of delivery, as midrashic tradition: exposition and application.

To the extent that the old Isaiah scroll was in the hands of learned men at a synagogue service, it may have happened that the people in the synagogue in the New Testament era had the text presented to themselves in a more clear and vibrant way than those who listened to it when it was read the first time. This is the case in spite of the fact that the written text had hardly been altered at all during the centuries since the book was written. Radical shift of medium or not, the question is not very simple!

In the synagogue service the problem of oral and written transmission was solved brilliantly; what solution could be more ingenious? The two media stood in very intimate interaction, the advantages of both were exploited and the disadvantages were reduced to a minimum.

I am not saying that the gospel tradition was handed on this way. My example from the Jewish milieu was chosen to show how complicated the relation between oral and written transmission can be; a simple model from oral cultures does not take us very far.

d. Fixed and flexible elements

There are very clear differences between spontaneous oral talking and a markedly written presentation, and it is very interesting to study them. But a simple distinction between orality and textuality does not solve many problems. Both oral and written delivery and transmission can appear in a thousand forms. Both can be flexible— not only the oral tradition; both can be fixed—not only the written tradition. And two of the most fascinating problems here are (1) what role the fixed elements play, and (2) the very interaction between these fixed elements and the great flexible, living part of the verbal tradition.

Although Kelber criticizes my principles forcefully, he offers a sympathetic and partly very good picture of my own approach (pp. 8–14); but curiously enough he fails to see the role of the flexible part of tradition and of the interplay between fixity and flexibility in my approach.[44] My starting point was the observation that although the ancient Jewish tradition was so rich, vibrant, flexible, and creative, in most contexts, yet many texts were transmitted with extreme care for the exact wording. Therefore my question was: where and how were texts reproduced without significant change? In other words, I indicated a *total* picture but concentrated my actual attention on *a specific part* of the whole.[45]

It is not true that "texts" only appear in written tradition or in traditions which are influenced by the written word. Nor is it true that all oral presentation is adapted to the listener and therefore constantly influenced by the situations of use. As for the ideal linguistic communication, it is of course a fact that the speaker's words are perfectly adapted to the listener and his situation, but this only happens when the speaker has unlimited freedom to choose his words himself. As soon as he tries to render what somebody else has said—reproduce the real utterance of this person—the possibilities of adapting his language to the listener are reduced. And the more he has reasons for giving a direct *quotation,* the less can he decide what wording his communication shall have. The one who will programmatically hand on verbal tradition has only limited freedom.

It is quite clear that the phenomenon we call a text—a self-contained, rounded utterance, shorter or longer, with a more or less fixed wording—has arisen in the *oral* stage of language. We may take the proverb as an example. Such a text has a very fixed wording indeed; even a very slight alteration brings about protests from the audience! And the proverb is clearly an *oral* text. There are written collections, but they are secondary. There are proverbs formulated

---

[44] See especially *Memory,* 19–21, 41–42, 71–78, 79–84.
[45] Ibid., 19–32, 33–42, 71–78.

by some writer, but they are imitations. We also know of other oral texts with a very fixed wording: certain types of songs and poems, certain sacred texts, legal texts, genealogies, and so forth. Not least interesting are those texts that are handed on in spite of the fact that the transmitter himself does not understand the words he is reciting from memory.[46]

Therefore it seems to me that we cannot possibly accept the simplified view that oral communication is always a flexible communication, the firmest elements of which are certain standardized expressions and formulas and other clichés, motifs, plots, certain linguistic devices, and the like. And it is quite clear that we do not get very helpful models from this type of orality for our study of early Christianity and its mother-tradition in antiquity.

On the other hand, it is extremely important to investigate the *interaction* between the fixed and the flexible elements in tradition, especially the text and commentary model. This applies to different types of oral tradition and different individual texts with an oral prehistory. But it also applies to written tradition. Written texts were often changed in antiquity, at least a little, but more important is the fact that they were transformed into an oral presentation when they were read and thereby usually received support from additional, flexible oral language. As long as written documents were hardly more than an aid to oral presentation, declamations and readings were connected with clarifying oral elements. When anyone in antiquity read a book aloud for others, the reader or some other expert had to be prepared for questions: the obscurities of the text were to be mastered by rereading, clarifications, comments, and perhaps exposition.[47] Our own perfectly printed book pages cause us to miss historical realities of this kind.

Kelber's main interest is not history but rather language and literary phenomena.[48] I do not find much about the behavioral, institutional, and material dimensions of tradition in his approach. In

---

[46] Ibid., 123–36.

[47] Even the classical procedure of the grammarian, who taught children to read texts, is revealing. It included four elements: criticism of the text *(diorthōsis)*, reading *(anagnōsis)*, explication *(exēgēsis)*, and judgment *(krisis);* cf. ibid., 124–25.

[48] *The Oral and the Written Gospel* (n. 36), 18; cf. 8 and 70–77.

fact his model—orality vs. textuality—does not seem to harmonize very well with the historical realities we glimpse in our sources. In the New Testament, Jesus of Nazareth is nowhere presented as a popular "performer" who entertains crowds with oral narratives or oral poetry of the type folklorists often mention. He has original traits but he is classified as a teacher and a prophet *(didaskalos, prophētēs)*—and more than a teacher and a prophet (cf. below, sect. 7).[49] It is said that he preaches and teaches *(kēryssein, didaskein)* and that he heals sick people and exorcizes demons. It seems very odd to me to put Jesus in the category where the folklorists place their oral narrators and oral poets.

Our sources also tell us that Jesus used to teach with the aid of parables *(parabolai/meshālim)*.[50] In the ancient Jewish texts we see that Hebrew word *māshāl* is a very broad designation which can be used for a long series of different linguistic creations. But these have three things in common: (1) they are texts (oral texts primarily, but also written ones)—not free streams of words; (2) they are brief— not whole books; and (3) they have an artistic design—they differ from bland everyday speech.

Related to Jesus' custom of teaching with the aid of *parabolai* (let me call them *meshalim,* in the plural) is the fact that all items of the proper sayings-tradition from Jesus extant in the Synoptic Gospels, have the form of meshalim: the items are texts, they are brief, and they are artistically designed. This applies to the extremely short items (let me call them *logia*) and to the somewhat longer but still very short narrative parables. One can always discuss how to divide the speeches of Jesus in the Synoptic Gospels, but let us disregard differences in detail for the moment. In his book *Jesus als Lehrer,* Rainer Riesner divides the synoptic collections of sayings into 247 independent units. About 65 percent of these are not more than two verses long. Only 12 percent are longer than four verses.[51]

The possibility that this picture only reflects a late stage of transmission, when literacy and textuality had got control over a tra-

---

[49] See further Riesner, *Jesus als Lehrer* (n. 1), and cf. E. P. Sanders, *Jesus and Judaism* (London: SCM, 1985).

[50] Esp., Mark 4:2, 33–34; Matt 13:3, 34–35.

[51] Riesner, *Jesus als Lehrer,* 392–93.

dition which was oral and flexible in its first stage, seems to be quite unrealistic. There were fixed elements within the synoptic sayings tradition even from the beginning; a mashal is a mashal.

On the other hand, there was of course also a living, flexible exchange of words. The sources show not only that Jesus communicated meshalim but also that he was talking to people, answering questions, discussing, preaching, teaching, exhorting, etc. All this was, of course, not done exclusively in the form of meshalim.

We have observed the fact that the fixed text often needs commentary. This applies to texts of the mashal type to a special degree. When in the Gospels we see that Jesus must explain what he has said in a mashal, this need not be a secondary feature in the tradition. Nobody can express puzzling proverbs and enigmatic parables without being questioned or feeling himself that something needs explanation. Meshalim—most types of this variegated category—evoke curiosity, wonder, pondering, questions, discussions.[52]

As for the *narratives* about Jesus, a few exceptions may lead one to think of oral narration of the common popular type (flexible "composition in transmission"). Martin Dibelius called these narratives tales *(Novellen)* and regarded them as more secular *(weltlich)* than the other material and more secondary as well. He also thought that these narratives had not been in use in early Christian preaching as had the other narratives but that they stemmed from special "narrators."[53] On this point Dibelius has attracted very few followers. Kelber now puts forward the thesis that the pre-Markan narrative material in its entirety comes from oral narration of the common popular type.

A thorough analysis of the entire narrative material in the synoptic tradition will reveal to what extent a thesis of this kind can stand the test. But I do not think this model is very adequate as to narrative tradition either. Our sources from early Christianity do not say a word about narrators of this type. And what we meet in the bulk of the synoptic narrative tradition is texts which very briefly and schematically present single episodes from the activity of Jesus.

---

[52] From this point of view note, e.g., Mark 4:10, 34; 7:17; 8:16–17; 9:32; 10:10, 24, 26; 13:14.

[53] *Die Formgeschichte des Evangeliums* (2d ed.; Tübingen: Mohr [Siebeck], 1933), 66–100, esp. 66–67, 94–100; ET *From Tradition to Gospel* (trans. B. L. Wolfe; New York: Scribner's Sons, 1934), 70–103, esp. 70–71, 91–103.

The presentation is usually so concentrated and terse that the wording does not allow much scope for variations. We read a brief description of the situation leading up to a saying of Jesus, a recording of a conversation with one or two rejoinders, or a brief account of a case of healing or exorcism. The superfluous words in a pericope of this kind are few, the margin for variation very small. It is difficult to see it otherwise than that these condensed narratives have been *texts* even at their oral stage, notwithstanding that the demand for unaltered wording has not been as strong in the narrative elements as in the sayings of Jesus in these texts. It is also easy to imagine that the *narrative* texts have been more readily influenced by the narrator's overall picture of Jesus and of his actual aim than are the sayings of Jesus.[54]

In his book, Werner Kelber stresses the importance of considering the social involvement of the gospel tradition (pp. 14–43 and passim). To him, however, the social factors occur primarily in the form of social pressure from the audience on the narrator. The presence and character of the audience, and the social surroundings of it, influence rather strongly the way the narrator formulates his presentation. Kelber characterizes my approach as "a model of passive transmission" and notes in my description "a virtual exemption of the oral Torah from active social engagement" (pp. 8–14). This is a misunderstanding. My view is that the Torah was a very vibrant factor in the Jewish milieu and that the gospel tradition belonged to the concrete existence of the Jesus movement and the early church, and was transmitted within the frame of the early Christian "work with the Word of the Lord."[55] In *Memory and Manuscript* I attempted to give a concrete picture of some aspects of this work with the Word, which, of course, was influenced by the social conditions of the teachers involved. Their way of collecting, selecting, formulating and reformulating, interpreting and expounding, grouping and regrouping the traditional texts does not go on without influence from their present situation: they are affected themselves, they take positions themselves, they get questions from others, and so on. Not even the most academic halakists among the rabbis were completely

---

[54] Cf. "The Path," sects. 7–8 (above).

[55] *Memory* (n. 2), 324–35; *Tradition* (n. 2), 37–47; *Origins,* sects. 12–13 (above), and "The Path," passim (above).

uninfluenced by the social life around them; such is the case even more so far as the haggadic teachers are concerned!

e. The origin and character of the gospel tradition

If Jesus was a child prodigy and if he was remarkable when growing up, it is possible that his family spread a sort of tradition about him already at that time, in free wording. But we can only speculate about this; in the Gospels the material from the time before Jesus began his public ministry is both scanty and fragile. The proper, specific early Christian tradition does not start until Jesus appears publicly before Israel.

(1) How can we imagine the beginning of the gospel tradition which records Jesus' preaching and teaching in *words*?

It starts when Jesus "opens his mouth and teaches" and gains sympathizers, adherents, and disciples, who accept his message. We have already underlined two basic facts: that our sources tell us that Jesus taught with the aid of short, artistically formulated texts, and that the extant material in the synoptic sayings tradition is a series of such texts. It is important to notice that the Synoptics use the same word for parables and logia (aphorisms): both are *parabolai (meshālim)*.[56] We must of course analyze the material more closely and categorize it more precisely for our aims, but it is interesting that the early Christian transmitters and evangelists did not see any difference in principle between logia and parables. Evidently they were transmitted in roughly the same way, even if it was easier to vary the wordings of a longer parable than in a brief proverbial logion.

These texts were presumably transmitted as memorized texts in roughly the same way as the Jewish mashal-tradition, with roughly the same technique as Jewish material of similar types (note that haggadic material normally had freer wording than halakic rules). I have tried to illustrate this in my previous writings on the subject,[57] and need not repeat myself here.

---

[56] Note how the word *parabolē* is used in most cases in the parable chapter (Mark 4:1–34; Matt 13:1–52; Luke 8:4–18); and cf. Mark 7:17; Matt 15:15; Luke 6:39. In Luke 4:23 the word means "proverb."

[57] In *Memory* I worked on the base of a very broad conception of the word "Torah." I did not take it in the narrow sense "law" but in its broadest

I have also stressed the fact that all verbal tradition has a very wide range of flexible words. This phenomenon is not, however, as interesting as are the fixed elements, since it is so general, so common, and so difficult to separate from everyday speech. But it is important to be aware of the fact that the verbal tradition does include this phenomenon and that it is a vital part of it: texts must very often be interpreted or expounded, especially if they have the form of puzzling logia or thought-provoking parables.[58]

I do not think I shall linger on this for the moment. But let me illustrate the phenomenon that the verbal tradition includes an interaction between elements of different character with an example I drew attention to in *Memory and Manuscript* (p. 145). In the parable chapter of Matthew (13:1–52) we find Jesus teaching with the aid of parables. In order to illuminate the different ways of receiving the message of the reign of heaven, Jesus relates to the people (1) the parable of the Sower (vv. 3–9). This is a text with a firm wording; the small margin of alteration can be measured by way of a comparison between the parallels. The content of the parable is also clarified (2) in the form of an interpretive exposition presented as complementary teaching for the disciples (vv. 10–23). The vocabulary is of another type in this exposition than in the parable itself, and many signs give us reason to think that these wordings were less fixed at the beginning than were the wordings of the parable. In the long run, however, they have become fixed as well. The parable is finally (3) treated as a well-known text with a name: *hē parabolē tou speirantos*, "the parable of the Sower" (v. 18). For the stranger this

---

meaning, as a collective designation for the Jews' sacred authoritative tradition in its entirety (cf. above n. 12). I also stressed the well-known fact that, within this circle, the haggadic material had normally a freer wording than the halakic rules, and the fact that "most of the gospel material is haggadic material," 335 (with reference to 96–97 and 146–48); see also 136–45, 177–81 and further *Tradition,* 33–37; *Origins,* sect. 12 (above), and "The Path," sect. 6 (above). Yet many critics have ascribed to me the view that Jesus was a Torah teacher in the meaning a "teacher of the law." When I say that Jesus was a "parabolist" (*moshel*) I only specify more precisely the wider designation "haggadist" (cf. *Origins,* sect. 12 (above). Kelber (*The Oral and the Written Gospel,* 38, n. 131) is mistaken when he takes this as a revocation of my earlier position (that Jesus was a "teacher of the law"!).

[58] See above, nn. 12 and 44.

name is an empty designation. But within the circle where this parable is a well-known text from Jesus, this name is a terse actualization of the parable and its message.[59]

Here we get a concrete example of the inner secrets of the verbal tradition. Explicit and implicit forms, exhaustive and concise versions, may exist side by side. A wealth of different forms is natural in a milieu where a certain verbal tradition is cultivated. One can quote a text verbally, or almost verbally; one can render it more freely, paraphrase it, or hand on its message in the form of an interpretation; one can condense it into a brief formula, even a name.[60] If we come across one of these forms we cannot conclude that the other forms did not exist for this author. To ask how much Paul knew of the concrete Jesus tradition—or in what forms he knew it—is not the same as studying direct quotations in the letters he occasionally wrote to particular communities.[61]

(2) As for *the mighty deeds* of Jesus the rumors certainly spread as soon as somebody was impressed by Jesus. But the inner circle within the Jesus movement and the church afterwards claimed to have more definite knowledge. During the time of Jesus there perhaps was no urgent reason for creating fixed texts about the mighty acts of the Master. Possibly, however, some such texts were needed when Jesus sent out his disciples to spread his message during his activity in Galilee; the traditions about this commissioning do not seem to be post-Easter fictions.[62] In Matt 11:4–6 and the parallels, we get an interesting picture of a situation in which some of John the Baptist's disciples are made transmitters of Jesus tradition to the Baptist. What occasional "Jesus propagandists" said about the Master (cf., e.g., Mark 1:45; 5:19–20) is not easy to know; their narration was hardly of the concise synoptic type.[63]

---

[59] Another example is the parable of the Tares in Matt 13: mashal (24–30), exposition (37–43), name (36); *Memory*, 145. We must also remember that pupils in the Hellenistic schools learned both to present a theme briefly and to develop it broadly (*brevitas, amplificatio*).

[60] See further *Memory*, 130–36, 171–81.

[61] *Memory*, 290–302, and *Origins*, sect. 7 (above). Cf. T. Holtz, "Jesus-Überlieferung und Briefliteratur," *Wissenschaftliche Zeitschrift, Univ. Halle* 34'85 G, H. 1 (1984): 103–12.

[62] E. E. Ellis, "New Directions in Form Criticism," 299–315, esp. 302–4.

[63] Note, however, Riesner, *Jesus als Lehrer* (n. 1), 487–88.

On the whole, I think we must conclude that the real need for brief, pointed narratives about the characteristic deeds of Jesus did not arise until after the departure of the Master, when the leadership shifted over from Jesus himself to others, above all the Twelve. When they preached and taught about Jesus as the Messiah, the Son of God, and discussed his secrets with each other and with opponents and critics, it certainly was not natural to confine themselves to the sayings of Jesus. And when they scrutinized the holy scriptures in order to understand the Jesus events better and find prophetic hints about him, it was perhaps near at hand to formulate brief texts about his most typical deeds and about other important episodes in his life on earth. Even these brief narrative texts were probably transmitted by way of memorization; *the primordial sayings-tradition set the pattern.*

(3) *The passion narrative* has certainly had a specific position from a very early time. In this case the events themselves were coherent; the moments came in rapid succession, not as isolated episodes, and the event as a whole cried out for another explanation than the official one that the authorities had silenced a deceiver *(planos)*. Here the adherents of Jesus needed an interpretation "from within" to set up against the official declarations of the outsiders. It is interesting to see that the passion narrative is a chain of episodes but that these—or most of them—belong intimately together, because they narrate and interpret a common chain of events.[64]

As for this decisive part of the Jesus tradition, the New Testament books are full of verbal presentations in the most different forms, from brief condensed formulas to extensive, freely worded expositions (the speeches in Acts, the letters).

f. The production of texts: creation, reshaping, compilation

In the discipline of New Testament studies we must often tackle problems which initially seem to be unsolvable but which eventually turn out to be possible to handle. Let me now mention a set of such questions.

---

[64]This ancient insight, stressed by the three pioneer form critics, has been strongly radicalized by R. Pesch in his commentary on the Gospel of Mark and in his book *Das Evangelium der Urgemeinde: Wiederhergestellt und erläutert von Rudolf Pesch* (Freiburg i.Br.: Herder, 1979). See also Pesch's impressive response to his critics, "The Gospel in Jerusalem: Mark

The form critics increased our sensitivity to the *forms* of the gospel material. Since then the achievements of redaction critics, composition critics, and text theorists of various schools have sharpened our sensitivity still more and given us even better instruments for discerning the form and anatomy of the synoptic texts. At present, text-pragmatic studies seem to be à la mode: one brings the intended addressees of the texts into focus and treats the texts as means of communication.

I think, however, that we can improve upon these analyses somewhat by working even more concretely than we usually do with some elementary *historical* questions concerning the very making of the New Testament texts: How did Jesus and early Christianity proceed, technically speaking, when they formulated and reformulated their texts? In my opinion, we need rather concrete ideas of the very process of creation, concerning both the individual texts and the text collections, including the final written gospels.

Generally speaking, I think we can isolate the creation of a text from its various uses, and fix the process of creation as an act in itself. We know that a text can arise suddenly through the prompting of the moment, in practical situations of various kind, but even then it is reasonable to ask how this came about. In most cases, however, the text is created outside the practical situations wherein it will be used, and the author is well aware of what happens in the process.[65] This applies especially to written texts.

Studies in the psychology of artistic inspiration[66] show that different authors give different answers to the question of how they create their texts. Some of them claim just to receive texts under strong inspiration; the poems come to them completed and perfect with meter, rhythm, rhyme, and everything, and need only to be written down. Others say that their texts, even those which give the impression of being strongly "inspired," are the result of hard intellectual labor. Yet others declare that the texts certainly come to them in

---

14:12–26 as the Oldest Tradition of the Early Church," *The Gospel and the Gospels* (n. 33), 106–48.

[65] See "The Path," sects. 3–4, 7–8 (above).

[66] T. Andræ, *Mystikens psykologi: Besatthet och inspiration* (2d ed.; Stockholm: Verbum, 1968), 176–444.

moments of inspiration but that they must nevertheless be revised
very thoroughly in order to stand. Of course there are many possibilities between the extremes here.

Now to our material. I cannot discuss every category of text and
all stages. Let me confine myself to three levels and to the main types
of synoptic texts.

Text creation. (1) How did the genuine *sayings* of Jesus originate? Was Jesus a man of strong inspiration who just "received"
his logia and parables? Or did he create them very consciously? In
the latter case, did he normally do so in contexts of conversation,
teaching, extemporaneous preaching, or other communal contexts? Or did he do it in solitude? Did he repeat his texts in order
to implant them firmly in his own memory? And what role did
the disciples play? Were they, as it were, his notebooks? Questions
of this kind may seem totally impossible now, and some of them
may even sound ridiculous, but they may become possible to deal
with once we have tried to come to grips with the process of text
creation.[67]

(2) How did the *episodal narratives* about Jesus originate? In this
case it is hardly realistic to think of a markedly inspirational process
of creation. Early Christian prophets did not present such texts.
They were certainly formulated very consciously. How? Did it take
place in a situation of teaching or discussion, so that someone in the
session had the task of formulating the text while the others listened
and suggested improvements until the text was finished and
accepted? Or did specific, skilled individuals always create such texts
individually, outside the situations of teaching or study? How did
that occur, to be precise? Were specific patterns consciously followed—Old Testament patterns, contemporary Jewish patterns,
more decidedly Hellenistic patterns? Was the form of the text chosen
with special regard to its *primary* use, that which the form critics call

---

[67] I have collected some concrete material for comparison in *Memory,*
esp. 130–36, 171–89. I also think that the present interest in the devices of
ancient rhetoric will help us in this connection. See, e.g., V. K. Robbins,
Jesus the Teacher: A Socio-Rhetorical Interpretation of Mark (Philadelphia:
Fortress, 1984).

its proper *Sitz im Leben*?[68] To what extent were notebooks used in this situation (the rabbinic material shows that such tools were not *necessary*)? The questions may be multiplied.

(3) Does the distinctiveness of the *passion narrative* warrant the supposition that it was created in some other way than the rest of the narrative traditions? In that case, how? Most of the episodes in the passion narrative are, as we know, self-contained units but at the same time natural links within the story at large: was this a result of conscious deliberation on the part of those who formulated the passion narrative? Were more or different people involved in the creation of this narrative than in the other cases? Was it written down earlier than the episodal stories, maybe even from the start? (It could function mainly as a memorized text, to be recited from memory just the same.)

Reshaping of texts. As for the transmission of the fixed texts, the methods of the transmitter and the receiver, I think I shall not repeat here what I have written in other connections. But a cluster of questions could be formulated concerning the deliberate reformulations of the fixed texts during the phase of transmission. In *Memory and Manuscript*[69] I offer some hints about the way in which transmitted texts were altered in the rabbinic schools and sessions, but I wish I had written more about that; it would have prevented the misunderstanding that the rabbis never changed their texts or that all types of rabbinic texts had the same fixed wording. Here, a good deal of work remains to be done if we want to understand how the variations in the fixed texts have arisen.[70]

Text compilation. At the stage of the creation of the large written gospels we have to ask how they were produced, technically

---

[68] For my part I do not think the text was actually formulated in the situation for which it was primarily intended to be used; see "The Path," sects. 3–4 and 7 (above).

[69] E.g., 77–78, 97–98, 103–12, 120–21, 152–53. Cf. also *Tradition*, 37–40.

[70] J. Neusner has now summarized his illuminating studies of the specific rabbinic methods of transmitting abbreviated halakic rules *(apodoseis)* in the Mishna in the book *The Memorized Torah: The Mnemonic System of the Mishnah* (BJS 96; Chico: Scholars Press, 1985).

speaking. How do we imagine that Mark, Matthew, Luke, John—let me call them so—actually proceeded, when they produced their famous books? Who were these evangelists, and how well-versed were they in the entire early Christian tradition? How well were they socialized in early Christianity's behavioral tradition, ethically, didactically, liturgically? What position did they have in the church seen as a kind of institution? (Did each of them, when writing his book, have the authority of a great apostle behind himself?) And how did this influence their writing? How familiar were they with the broad verbal tradition of the church? How much did they know of the oral textual tradition? How much did they have in the form of documents? How did they collect their material? Did they travel, search for collections, consult informants? And how did they actually proceed when compiling their books? Did they have the scrolls and codices in front of them? Did they know them more or less by heart? Did they feel a duty to copy visually from the columns in the Vorlagen or could they follow some freer model and adapt their texts in a more targumic way? Did they have in their memory oral versions of the pericopes present in their written sources, and, in such cases, did these versions have the same authority for them as the written versions? Did they use loose notes for the first phase of their attempts to combine their sources? Did they rewrite their drafts many times? Such questions are not unrealistic; I think we should try to find answers, at least for our own silent use. If we cannot form a concrete conception of the process of compiling the Gospels we have reason to surmise that something is wrong with our solution of the synoptic question and of many other related topics.

Moreover, if we come to grips with concrete questions of this kind, perhaps we can also formulate criteria for deciding whether a text has been created—or reworked—as an *oral* text or if it has been produced in *written* form. I do not think we have any proper criteria for this so far.

g. The synthesizing of the text material

According to Rudolf Bultmann,[71] the individual elements of the gospel tradition originated first, independently of each other,

---

[71] *Die Geschichte der synoptischen Tradition* (FRLANT 29; 2d ed.; Göttingen: Vandenhoeck & Ruprecht, 1931), 393–400; ET *History of the*

but it was "in the nature of the case" that they were gathered in collections which gradually became more extensive and finally were
written down. The synoptic evangelists were collectors and editors
rather than authors. Yet, Mark made a pioneer achievement when he
wrote his gospel as the first in the series. Here the loosely conglomer-
ated material was interpreted and organized along main lines taken
from the Christology and the kerygma of the Hellenistic church.

Kelber (pp. 44–89 and passim) objects that nothing in orality
makes writing natural. The narration about Jesus in Early Christianity
was by nature oral, pluriform, and multidirectional. When Mark
changed the flourishing tradition into a linear account and wrote it
down, new factors were decisive, in part pronouncedly antitraditional
factors (pp. 184–226).

I do not think we can get a realistic picture of the synthesizing
process if we do not consider all the dimensions of the early Christian tradition. This tradition was intraecclesiastical. The evangelists
were hardly very impressed by pluriform outsider rumors and multidirectional talk about Jesus among the people. But they were certainly very well acquainted with the insider tradition about him. In
the communities which arose around the message about Jesus
Christ, there was a new, enthusiastic belief in Jesus and a living interest in his person, spirit, and will. Here was an "inner tradition," a
spiritual atmosphere which repelled negative interpretations of Jesus
and cultivated positive ones. Certainly, opinions were divided in
some questions and various conflicts were unavoidable, but all who
got the floor had a positive overall picture of Jesus, his person, spirit,
and will, and at least a rough idea about his career and fate on earth.
Already in the inner tradition there was a certain unity: an attitude
toward Jesus which kept that which was said about him within a certain framework and gave it something of an organic unity.

To say this is to draw attention to the effects of "the institutional tradition" at the same time. Institutionalization had shown
itself in the fact that a borderline had arisen between insiders and
outsiders, impeding the influx of wild, foreign, or negative interpretations of Jesus. And as for the situation *intra muros:* those who had

---

Synoptic Tradition (trans. J. Marsh; Oxford: Blackwell, 1963; New York:
Harper & Row, 1968), 368–74.

the highest reputation as experts concerning what Jesus had said and done—especially those who could say that they had heard and seen for themselves—certainly had the best chances to set the tone as traditionists (cf., e.g., Acts 1; Gal 1–2; 1 John 1:1–4). This reduced the pluralism of the traditions about Jesus.

Even the programmatic "behavioral tradition" which was cultivated within the church was a synthesizing factor: a foreign body could hardly be tolerated. I am thinking of the imitation of Christ as a programmatic model for the Christian's lifestyle but also of liturgical, didactic, therapeutic, and exorcistic activity within the church. Here we have another unifying factor.

Turning to "the verbal tradition" one must remember that it not only contained a number of isolated quotations from Jesus and episodal narratives about him. There were also unifying and joining elements in this connection. Even the general usage of language in early Christianity—the flexible, variegated way of speaking about Jesus—formed very soon a certain vocabulary, formulas, motifs, etc., which became typical. These observations remind us that the synthesizing of the gospel was not something entirely secondary. *Intra muros* the Jesus tradition was in certain respects always something of a unity, stamped by the same deeply devotional attitude to Jesus. Thus, we are moving *within a frame of unity* when we pose the question of how the very texts about Jesus were synthesized into orderly accounts *(diēgēseis)* and became written gospels.

The transmitted texts contained elements which were summaries and thus paved the way for a natural organization of the concrete texts. I am thinking of verbal elements which either classify and characterize the person of Jesus or briefly summarize and categorize his "works." In the former case, I aim at such designations as (our) Teacher, the Prophet, Messiah/Christ, God's Son, the Lord, and the like. These titles characterized the person of Jesus and did so *together;* we know of no early Christian group which could classify Jesus with the aid of only one existing title. In this way a complex but coherent picture of Jesus' person was built up. In early Christianity all these designations have two things in common: they all characterize *Jesus of Nazareth* and they do so in a positive and majestic way. Low or negative designations are not accepted. In the long run, these intraecclesiastical titles of Jesus become virtually synonymous;

they all function to denote the whole Jesus. This is a telling example of their synthesizing and unifying character. The concrete Jesus tradition deals almost solely with the man who receives these titles.[72]

In the latter case I have in mind the fact that it was impossible already at the beginning to be content with only individual, episodal narratives about the activity of Jesus. Even from the first moment one had sometimes to be brief. Already when Jesus had preached and taught a couple of times, the disciples and others must have been able to say briefly that Jesus "preached and taught." After a while they could certainly claim that he "preached and taught about the reign of God." In the same way they must have been able to state in general words, after having seen a couple of mighty acts, that Jesus "cured sick people and cast out demons." Such verbal elements are *unavoidable* in every linguistically developed milieu. We may have different opinions about the factual summaries to be found in the Synoptic Gospels, whether in their present form they are formulated by the evangelist or not. But it would be foolish to think that there was no need for summarizing items of this kind before the written organization of the material.

In this way we can analyze the various parts of the text tradition and observe how the different elements contain items which could help anyone who wanted to organize the material into an orderly account to find a basis for his arrangement. Let me mention a few more examples. Some traditions contained certain geographic or chronological information. Rightly or wrongly, these could offer complementary knowledge for dating or localizing other traditions lacking such information. Of great interest are retrospective or forward-pointing elements, for instance Jesus' words about his mighty deeds (Matt 11:20–24 and parallels) or his predictions about the passion and resurrection (Mark 8:31 and all the parallels). Elements of this kind facilitate synthesis and organization of the material. Traditions about a conflict between Jesus and his opponents included a natural relationship to the final intervention against him. And the

---

[72] On Jesus as "the only teacher," see *Memory*, 332–33; *Tradition*, 40–43; *Origins*, sect. 8 (above), and "The Path," sects. 1–4 (above). [See now further, S. Byrskog, *Jesus the Only Teacher: Didactic Authority and Transmission in Ancient Israel, Ancient Judaism, and the Matthean Community* (ConBNT 24; Stockholm: Almqvist & Wiksell International, 1994).]

passion narrative made it natural to look for reasons for this condemnation, and for evidence of the innocence of Jesus as well, in the traditions about his prior teaching and mighty deeds.[73]

I mentioned *the passion narrative.* It has undoubtedly played an eminent role as a first step toward a synthetic, complete gospel. Here, an important part of the history of Jesus was narrated rather early in the form of an orderly account. It is easy to understand that this coherent presentation of the *decisive* part of Jesus' work called for a substructure, a complementary introduction. Martin Kähler's well-known description of the Gospel of Mark as a "passion narrative with an extended introduction" indicates how the evangelist got his most impressive idea for the disposition of his composition.

I break off here. My contention is that a coherent account of "all that Jesus began to do and teach" did not exist at the beginning of early Christianity and that the first one who wrote a gospel (I think it was Mark) certainly was a pioneer; yet, *his achievement was hardly very creative.* He had good text material, he did not need to reinterpret it very much, nor change its form very much; even the disposition of the material was near at hand. His achievement was that he actually did what many others could also have done, but that he did it so connaturally with the material that his followers had no reason for constructing a disposition of quite another type.

h. The process of writing down

I have already pointed out that the concrete Jesus tradition arose in a milieu strongly influenced by the holy scriptures; these were "alive" through actual reading, translation, interpretation, and application. During the whole time from Jesus to the evangelists, the gospel tradition had natural connections with a verbal mother-tradition within which the written word played an important role.

---

[73] It is, however, very interesting to note that the opposition against Jesus' bold way of forgiving sins (Matt 9:1–8 and parr.), his exorcisms (Matt 9:32–34; 12:22–24 and parr.) and his healings on the sabbath (e.g., Matt 12:9–14 and parr.) has not been taken into account explicitly in the passion narrative in spite of the fact that all three of these points could be classified as capital crimes (a more lenient interpretation was of course also possible).

On the other hand, it is very striking that Jesus himself did not write. He was a man who spoke. He talked to people, he preached orally, taught orally, did mighty acts with his oral word, etc. Only in one place do our sources mention that he wrote something (John 8:6), but that was on the ground and nobody knows what it was. Nothing indicates that Jesus wrote down one single logion, parable, or speech. Nor is it indicated anywhere that he incited disciples or others to write or that he dictated to them. The verbal tradition that Jesus himself initiated, was *oral.*

As for the disciples, it is nowhere mentioned that they took notes or carried notebooks. They "are with" Jesus, they "follow" him, they are his "disciples," they "hear and see," they recollect, and they sometimes question Jesus about something he has said or done. Thus the disciples have seen and heard, they remember, ponder, and discuss Jesus and his words and deeds. When the sole master suddenly has departed, the Jesus movement must be reconstructed and consolidated, a process the sociological consequences of which we can guess only to a certain degree. Nothing indicates, however, that the adherents of Jesus immediately change the medium of communication. They do not sit down in order to write a monograph about Jesus, a book to be duplicated and distributed. They do what we may expect disciples in this milieu to do: they continue in the footsteps of their master, they follow his aims, his behavior and teaching, and perhaps even direct instructions given; they carry on his work along his characteristic lines. What Acts and other New Testament writings say or reflect seems to be very probably true, namely, that the disciples of Jesus preach and teach in the name of Jesus and about Jesus, they heal sick people and expel demons in the name of Jesus, etc.[74] This is not strange at all, especially if earlier they had had the task of helping the Master in his work. That the new situation forces them to ponder and discuss more seriously than before the person and work of Jesus, especially his death, goes without saying; that they have much stronger reasons now than before for scrutinizing the holy scriptures in order to gain clarity, is easy to imagine. Of course nothing hampers them from taking various new steps as well; not

---

[74] See, e.g., Acts 4:17, 18; 5:28, 40; 9:27, 28; and 3:6; 4:7, 10, 30; 16:18.

least their strong conviction that the crucified Jesus is risen and that the Spirit is with them inspires them to new initiatives.

We do not get many indications about the role of writing in this connection. It is possible that notes and notebooks were taken into use early at this time; our sources are, alas, completely silent about it. Even less do we find anywhere an exhortation to use such means. We might, however, imagine that some such writing was done quite informally, for practical reasons; in that case it is no mystery that our sources do not mention it. But it is not at all self-evident. Even less is it true that early Christianity relied upon the written word.[75] If we look at the words and expressions used to characterize the verbal activity of Jesus and early Christianity, they do not exclude written means but neither does any of them give a clear or even natural hint at the use of written notes which were read aloud. Such words as *kēryssein, didaskein, homilein, dialegesthai, parakalein, nouthetein,* etc., aim primarily at an oral activity, not at a written one.

However, it can hardly be doubted that notebooks began to be used when the collections became more extensive than in the earliest period. But suddenly, and within a short period of time, from the late sixties onwards, written gospels appeared within the church. We do not know how many they were, only that four of them very easily forced out the other ones. It is rather difficult to explain this transition to written gospels. Probably many factors were intertwined and none of them alone was decisive.

We have to do with two questions: Why was the text material gathered into extensive collections? And why were these collections now properly *written down?*

The first question is not difficult to answer. What we call a "collecting mania" is a hypertrophy of a general human proclivity: what we find interesting and useful we save and gather, be it stamps, anecdotes, knowledge, or whatever. It is not difficult to understand that those in early Christianity who had to use the concrete Jesus tradi-

---

[75] Thus Neusner, *Rabbinic Traditions* (n. 12), vol. 3, 54. The gospel tradition was after all not written down immediately, and Paul could not possibly regard his oral teaching as less important or reliable than his letters. He only wrote letters when he could not come in person.

tions more than others, collected such texts; both interest and necessity forced them to do so. It was natural as well that structured collections of this kind emerged and expanded. Even the will to remember leads us to a conscious gathering and grouping of memory material. It is a precaution against forgetfulness. Other factors contributed as well, not least the needs of the communities. It is easy to imagine that notebooks were more and more taken into use in this work with the texts. Great synthetic collections of the same type as the Q collection or the Gospel of Mark are thus "in the nature of the case." And proper books had to come, sooner or later.

The Q collection hardly had such a well-structured disposition as did the Gospel of Mark. This gospel is not merely an extensive notebook *(hypomnēma)*. The author shows a desire to write for others, and his desire has taken him a step further than collecting material in a big notebook; he has arranged his texts in accordance with an overall view of Jesus and his work. On the other hand, the Gospel of Mark may not be a proper book *(ekdosis)* in all respects, written for common use.[76] The Gospel of Matthew, for its part, is a book in the more strict sense of the word, even if it was not written for the public market. It was presumably intended for a church province, maybe for the church everywhere. The Lukan writings seem to be written primarily for individual, cultivated Christians but probably for cultural outsiders as well. The Gospel of John gives the impression of having been designed for communities in the Johannine church province.

Why this remarkable writing? To some extent it may have happened by accident: local conditions in the community where the first of the evangelists wrote or the personal qualities of the evangelist may have occasioned the writing of the first gospel. With the model given and the first literary attempt made, the undertaking was copied by others in early Christianity. It is also a striking fact

---

[76] On the differences between properly published books and written notes, see V. Burr, "Editionstechnik," *Reallexikon für Antike und Christentum* 4 (1959): 597–10. For Jewish material, cf. S. Lieberman, *Hellenism in Jewish Palestine* (New York: Jewish Theological Seminary of America, 1950), 83–99. See also the discussion in *The Relationships among the Gospels: An Interdisciplinary Dialogue* (ed. W. O. Walker Jr.; San Antonio: Trinity University Press, 1978), 123–92.

that the Synoptics belong together. They are not three independent eruptions of creativity; they have vital causes in common.

The fact that time went on was also a factor, in itself. "The beginning" and the first "fathers" thereby got their patina. It is always difficult for the present and the authorities of the present to gain the acknowledgement, prestige, and authority of the fathers and the good old days. In this case the personal disciples of Jesus—especially the Twelve—had furthermore an immense authority as eyewitnesses, both because they had the reputation of having been authorized by Jesus himself, the Risen One, and because they had such a position within the church. It is easy to understand that the death of these pillars and other eyewitnesses sharpened the demand for the legacy to be preserved carefully and to be committed to writing.

Neither is it impossible that some of these fathers, Peter for instance, had something to do themselves with the matter. Peter may have given Mark occasion to write, or even urged him to do so, before his own death.

Another natural guess is that the progressive institutionalization and consolidation of the church made it desirable to have better books than before for the different needs of the communities.

Concrete events outside the church might have played their role as well, especially the fall of Jerusalem and the destruction of the temple in A.D. 70.[77] We know what a catastrophe this was to the Jews and what strivings for consolidation it evoked. The Christian sources do not give us reason to believe that the fate of Jerusalem in the year 70 shook early Christianity as much as Judaism, but it is reasonable to presume (1) that even those Jews who had become Christians were influenced by this catastrophe and its immediate consequences: the holy city and the temple could no longer be what they had been; (2) that the Palestinian authorities of early Christianity could no longer have the same influence as before in the church while other Christian centers gained greater influence; (3) that the fact that *Judaism* after the fall of the temple consolidated itself hastened early Christianity's consolidation with defense and counterattacks against the mother-religion. In these ways the fate of Jerusalem

---

[77] Cf. Kelber, *The Oral and the Written Gospel* (n. 36), 210–11.

and the temple may have affected the work with the Jesus tradition in Christian centers and contributed to the origin of solid, written gospels.

i. The polyphonic character of the written gospel

The early church was not only a number of independent congregations. There was also a common sense of unity: we are the church of Christ. A sign of this is the fact that the Gospels were so quickly distributed to other communities. They were *commune bonum* for the Christians.

A classical point in the discussion about the Fourth Gospel is the question of whether this gospel was written to complete the other gospels or to replace them. This question is, however, pertinent for each one of the Synoptic Gospels as well. And it is important: Was this book written in order to be *the* Gospel in a community or was it written in order to function as one of many voices in a choir? Only if we know for sure that an evangelist intended his book to be the exclusive gospel for his community can we take his book as a full presentation of his own total view. If he was writing in order to enrich existing collections and/or gospels, it is not unlikely that he could *presuppose* very much and allow himself a one-sidedness in his selection of material and in his emphases which he might otherwise have avoided.

Let me just hint at a few points. In the *Gospel of John* we easily see which disciple is the ideal one in the Johannine church: the Beloved Disciple. But Peter and the Twelve are not rejected. We may suspect criticism against them, but their authority is respected. We get a similar impression in the notices in 20:30–31, and 21:24–25, the words about the selection the evangelist has made from the Jesus tradition. Nothing here indicates that the Gospel of John was intended to be the only acceptable gospel. The spirit in these notices is not exclusive. The Gospel of John has not come to displace but to complete the others.

In the *Lukan* prologue we cannot with certainty read any criticism against Luke's predecessors. If Luke reproaches them, he does so in an almost indiscernible way. He reveals no wish to displace other gospels. What he says clearly is that his book will fulfil a special function which obviously the other "orderly accounts" he knows cannot fulfil. The Lukan writings are intended to be used as a complement to other gospels. Therefore, we cannot presume that Luke presents everything he accepts concerning Jesus in his gospel.

The author of the *Matthew* does not say one explicit word about himself and his informants. In the finale of the book (28:16–20) we read, however, that Jesus gives his disciples the command to teach all nations "to observe all that I have commanded you." Certainly this has in view not only sayings of Jesus of a commanding character but the authoritative Jesus tradition in its entirety. We get the impression that the Gospel of Matthew is intended to be as complete as possible concerning the concrete Jesus tradition. It shall be a comprehensive instrument for all tasks which the Risen One has given his church. On the other hand, it is not likely that Matthew thinks he has collected *everything* in his book and that, therefore, this gospel shall replace the other collections of Jesus tradition. We can see how Matthew uses the Gospel of Mark (I think he does). The latter is almost totally swallowed up; the *material* in the book of Mark becomes almost superfluous now. The same applies to the Q collection. But, even though Matthew reworks his two main sources in this way, he treats the material in them with a striking respect. Nowhere does he reveal suspicion or negativism against his sources or their authors. Therefore he certainly has not wanted to silence the oral tradition, refute the older collections or dispatch the Gospel of Mark to the *geniza*. The Gospel of Matthew is not written in an exclusive spirit. The evangelist stood in a tradition, in which Kings and Chronicles could stand side by side and a scriptural verse could be interpreted in many ways by one and the same teacher. Matthew certainly would not mind that the vivid Gospel of Mark continued to be used.[78]

It is not easy to know how *Mark* thought of earlier materials concerning the words and deeds of Jesus. Like Matthew, he finds no need to say a word about himself or his work. For my part I think that Mark has no intention to write a complete account of Jesus' words and deeds—"all about Jesus"—or to replace other attempts. Nor do I believe the many new hypotheses about his severe polemics

---

[78] The fact that the Gospel of Mark actually did come to be overshadowed by Matthew's Gospel is another matter.

against the family of Jesus, the Twelve, early Christian prophets and whatever.[79] To me it seems probable that Mark knows about the Q collection and *respects* it. Nothing indicates that Mark was so abnormal that he held the sayings of Jesus in contempt. He simply makes a narrow selection. The limited space he gives the sayings material in his book (some 27 percent of the total text) might very well have the explanation that there already existed a good and respectable collection which Mark wanted neither to integrate into his own presentation nor to replace. If the abrupt ending of Mark's Gospel is not due to some external, accidental fact—that one or two leaves are missing or that the evangelist's work was interrupted or that he wanted to write one more volume like Luke without being able to do so—it might have the explanation that the resurrection narratives were very well known texts, which perhaps even had a prominent place in the eucharistic liturgy. This is a hypothetical guess but hardly more far-fetched than a lot of other arguments from silence concerning the Gospel of Mark.

The Synoptic Gospels have a very simple canon history. This is easy to explain. They were rooted in the same tradition: they stemmed from circles whose members obviously knew each other rather well; as literary works they originated in connection with each other and were not written in order to displace each other. It was only natural that in many communities they were added to one another immediately in the beginning. The fact that they seem to have got a flying start in the church and enjoyed uncontested authority from the very beginning presumably means that they came from leading Christian authorities and centers. In the competition with other orderly accounts they were victorious; the fight was scarcely hard. It was a matter of the survival of the fittest but also dependent on certain privileges: these three did not have to fight each for himself; they belonged together and had a common authority.

The written gospel of the church is a polyphonic gospel—or tetraphonic gospel. This is not an entirely secondary fact, simply due to the recording of the gospel tradition and the inclusion of four records in a canon. To some extent it is even founded in the fact that

---

[79] Thus Kelber, *The Oral and the Written Gospel*, esp. 90–105, with references.

the oral gospel tradition *intra muros ecclesiae* was a plurality with a considerable homogeneity, and the fact that the evangelists did not intend to silence each other. It soon became difficult in the church to keep the witnesses of the different evangelists apart.[80] This is irritating to us New Testament scholars today, when we work hard at discerning the distinctive profile of each book as clearly as possible. But the four evangelists could certainly have written as Paul did: "Whether then it is I or they, so we preach, and so you believed" (1 Cor 15:11).[81]

j. Holy writ and viva vox

The spoken and the written word both have their advantages and their disadvantages. This subject is very fascinating. From before the era of perfectly printed books and rapid, silent reading, we have many utterances on this problem. Well known are Plato's words about the stupid written book, which can do nothing but repeat the same words, and the early Christian fathers' appreciative testimonies about the living voice in contrast to books.[82] Martin Luther took up this theme in a remarkable way, insisting on the principle that the gospel *(das Evangelium)* is not holy scriptures but a living, sounding word: *viva vox.*[83]

---

[80] Cf. H. Merkel, *Die Pluralität der Evangelien als theologisches und exegetisches Problem in der Alten Kirche* (Traditio christiana 3; Bern & Frankfurt a.M.: Peter Lang, 1978).

[81] The generous attitude expressed in Phil 1:18 is also telling.

[82] Plato, *Phaedrus,* 274b–78a; cf. *Epist.* 2 (314) and 7 (340–42). On different aspects of the problem of oral and written delivery in antiquity and in the ancient church, see H. von Campenhausen, *Kirchliches Amt und geistliche Vollmacht in den ersten drei Jahrhunderten* (BHT 14; Tübingen: Mohr [Siebeck], 1953), 221–33; ET *Ecclesiastical Authority and Spiritual Power in the Church of the First Three Centuries* (trans. J. A. Baker; Peabody, Mass.: Hendrickson, 1997), 201–12; L. Vischer, "Die Rechtfertigung der Schriftstellerei in der Alten Kirche," *Theologische Zeitschrift* 12 (1956): 320–36; E. F. Osborn, "Teaching and Writing in the First Chapter of the Stromateis of Clement of Alexandria," *Journal of Theological Studies* NS 10 (1959): 335–43, and H. Karpp, "Viva vox," *Mullus: Festschrift Theodor Klauser* (ed. A. Stuidber and A. Hermann; *Jahrbuch für Antike und Christentum* Erg.-band 1; Münster i.W.: Aschendorff, 1964), 190–98. Cf. also n. 37 above.

[83] See R. Prenter, *Spiritus creator: Studier i Luthers teologi* (2d ed.; Copenhagen: Samlerens Forlag, 1946), 127–37.

In the preceding I have rejected much in Werner Kelber's book, *The Oral and the Written Gospel.* His approach is based on an all too simple contrast between the spoken and the written word, between orality and written delivery (textuality). Nonetheless, I think his mobilizing of observations from Anglo-American folkloristic studies of orality—particularly if this category is taken in a more pluralistic way[84]—is valuable: from here the New Testament debate can be vitalized in questions concerning the gospel tradition and hermeneutics. In fact, Kelber's ambition is not only to elucidate the relation between the oral and the written gospel, but also, at the same time, to clarify the "oral psychodynamics" and to work out an "oral hermeneutic" as a complement to the usual hermeneutic, which he calls a textual one.

I am afraid I cannot follow Kelber very far in these points either. Yet I think his subjects are important. Jesus and early Christianity presented their own, new, specific message—from the eruptive center of their inner tradition—in oral forms first of all, and did so in a cultural setting where writings were never far away. This means that the transition to a stage where the oral gospel had basically become one or many books was not a superficial, technical triviality. Granted this significant change did not occur immediately when the Gospels were written (the oral tradition and the oral activity in other forms continued), something had started which in the long run would have important consequences. One hundred years later the written gospels had attained the stature of holy scripture and of primary sources for the Christian message. This process is a captivating object for historical study. But it also has deep theological and existential implications. It concerns themes that are among the greatest realities of the church: law and gospel, holy writ and *viva vox evangelii.*

---

[84] A good example is R. Finnegan, *Oral Poetry: Its Nature, Significance, and Social Context* (Cambridge: Cambridge University Press, London, New York, Melbourne, 1977), and idem, *Oral Literature in Africa* (Oxford: Clarendon, 1970).